HOW TO TAKE A
ROADTRIP
BY WAYNE HOFFMAN

T5-CGB-929

FODOR'S TRAVEL PUBLICATIONS
NEW YORK   TORONTO   LONDON   SYDNEY   AUCKLAND

How to Take a Road Trip

Editors: Karen Cure, Mark Sullivan, Jennifer Paull
Editorial Contributors: Lisa S. Kahn, Gary McKechnie
Production/Manufacturing: Robert B. Shields
Creative Director: Fabrizio LaRocca
Text and Cover Design: Guido Caroti
Cover Photo: Peter Guttman

Copyright

First Edition
ISBN 1–4000–1240–6
ISSN 1541–2881

Important Tip

All details in this book are based on information supplied to us at
press time. But changes occur all the time in the travel world, and
Fodor's cannot accept responsibility for facts that become outdated
or for inadvertent errors or omissions. **So always confirm specifics
as you plan your packing.** Specifically, call your airline to confirm
baggage limitations and your outfitter or tour operator to confirm
any must-haves for your trip.

Special Sales

Fodor's Travel Publications are available at special discounts for
bulk purchases for sales promotions or premiums. Special editions,
including personalized covers, excerpts of existing guides, and cor-
porate imprints, can be created in large quantities for special needs.
For more information, contact your local bookseller or write to
Special Markets, Fodor's Travel Publications, 1745 Broadway,
New York, NY 10019. Inquiries from Canada should be directed
to your local Canadian bookseller or sent to Random House of
Canada, Ltd., Marketing Department, 2775 Matheson Boulevard
East, Mississauga, Ontario L4W 4P7. Inquiries from the United
Kingdom should be sent to Fodor's Travel Publications, 20
Vauxhall Bridge Road, London SW1V 2SA, England.

PRINTED IN THE UNITED STATES OF AMERICA
10 9 8 7 6 5 4 3 2 1

Contents

On the Road

Would Jack Kerouac be famous if he'd written a book called "On the Train" instead of "On the Road"? If Willie Nelson sang a song called "On the Plane Again" instead of "On the Road Again," would anyone have listened to his record? Of course not. There's something magical about the prospect of hitting the road. It beckons with the promise of something new, something better just over the horizon. It's the ultimate symbol of a people on the go, ever moving yet always connected, regardless of time or distance.

There's nothing like a road trip to help you understand the magic of the open road. What better way to feel free than to toss an overnight bag in your backseat and take off for the weekend on a moment's notice? What better way to strengthen family bonds than to pack your kids in the minivan and drive to Grandma's house for a week? What better way to really see America than to hop in a motor home and spend a whole month visiting town after town, state after state?

Once you get behind the wheel, you'll understand how a road trip is a unique kind of journey, where getting there is as much fun as being there. Planes are efficient for covering long distances in a short time, but you miss more than you see along the way. Trains have a certain romance, but they limit your choice of destinations—you can't go where the tracks don't lead. Road trips offer opportunities that you simply can't get in other modes of transportation.

INCREDIBLE JOURNEYS

Aside from the intangibles, road trips have plenty of practical advantages over other kinds of travel. Most significantly, they're cheaper. Chances are good that you've already got a vehicle in your driveway. If not, renting one isn't a major expense compared to paying for plane or train tickets. When you're on the road, you'll easily be able to locate places to sleep and eat that'll fit any budget. If you're visiting family, such expenses will be even lower.

It's also simpler to plan a road trip, even on short notice. You don't have to worry that all the seats in your car will be sold out a month in advance, or that you won't have time to make a connection in Dallas, or that you'll be socked with a huge surcharge if you don't make reservations 14 days ahead of time. If your car is parked outside, you could take a trip right now.

Flexibility is the hallmark of road travel. You make the plans, and you can change them. You decide where to sleep, when to eat, and what to see. Want to stay at the Grand Canyon an extra day? No problem. Want to make an unplanned stop along your route? It's up to you. Feel like sleeping late and leaving town at noon instead of 8 AM? You're not locked into someone else's timetable—you're in charge. You can go wherever you like, whenever you like. Try that on a plane.

On a personal level, road travel offers a sense of togetherness that's hard to duplicate. When was the last time you spent a whole afternoon playing word games with your kids? How long has it been since you and your spouse had even one hour without interruptions from the telephone, television, or work? A road trip is a group outing where everyone is involved, a project you can plan together.

FORWARD THINKING

For most of us, a road trip requires considerable planning. But you shouldn't let that stop you. Planning can seem like a burden, but it's also an opportunity. You've got the freedom to create exactly the kind of trip you want to take. With a road trip—more so than any other kind of travel—you have control over almost every aspect of your journey.

Planning a trip isn't just about deciding where you want to go. It's also about deciding how you want to get there and what you want to see along the way. Pick a route that suits your tastes and a vehicle that's practical for the journey you're taking. Pack well, so you won't find yourself missing anything while you're away from home. Figure out how to keep everyone in your car—including kids, pets, and, most importantly, the driver—happy during the ride. Consider where you're going to spend the nights. Once you've got all these details planned, you're ready to hit the road.

No matter how much you plan, though, you can't control everything. You'll need to be prepared for mishaps, too, in case something goes wrong. With some forethought, you won't let a carsick child, anxious dog, or a flat tire stop you cold. You won't even lose your composure when faced with a driver's nightmare: getting lost.

Take time to consider every aspect of your journey from the moment you leave your home to the moment you return. Then, when you've got it all planned out, you can feel confident when you get behind the wheel and buckle your seat belt. This is going to be one heck of a ride.

PLANNING POINTS

While these topics are discussed fully in subsequent chapters, the following points should get your gears turning:

☐ If you're considering renting a vehicle, look into your options well ahead of time. Find out if your car insurance covers rentals, or what your credit card might cover, and supplement as needed.

☐ If you're driving your own car, schedule a full checkup with a mechanic. Check on the condition of your spare tire, and make sure the owner's manual is in the glove compartment.

☐ Obtain and study maps and guidebooks.

☐ If you're planning on traveling internationally, find out exactly what documentation you'll need, how your health insurance will cover your travels, and whether any foods are forbidden from crossing the border.

☐ If you have a cell phone, switch to a roaming plan. Get an adaptor so that you can charge the phone in your car. If you don't have a cell phone, consider renting or buying one for your trip.

☐ If you have a pet and are not taking it with you, make arrangements for its care while you're away. If you're taking a pet with you, schedule a checkup at the vet and review your pet-travel gear.

- ☐ Check your auto supplies and repair kit and fill in any gaps. Make sure you have an extra set of car keys.

- ☐ Consider where you'd like to stay and make lodging reservations as necessary.

- ☐ If you're staying with friends or family, ask them what you should bring (extra linens, etc.).

- ☐ Assess your luggage and get any essential new bags.

- ☐ Arrange for plant care and a mail and newspaper delivery hiatus if necessary.

Within a week of departure:

- ☐ Prepare navigator's materials.

- ☐ Thoroughly clean your vehicle.

- ☐ Stock up on food, drink, surprises for your kids, and any other perishables you'll be bringing.

- ☐ Tally toiletries, glove compartment items, and little extras; pick up anything that's missing.

- ☐ Gather music, games, and other in-car diversions.

- ☐ Do laundry and dry cleaning.

- ☐ Do practice runs: carrying your packed suitcases, attaching items to a car rack, loading your trunk.

- ☐ Decide on a driving schedule.

- ☐ Just before you go, check weather reports for your route and destination.

GO YOUR OWN WAY

In the movies, it's easy to be spontaneous. People pick places to travel by spinning a globe and stopping it with their index finger. Five minutes later, they've grabbed a tooth-brush and the perfect mix tape and they're on the road in their convertible enjoying another wacky adventure.

People in the movies wake up with perfect hair and fresh breath, too. Life is definitely not a movie.

For most of us, a road trip takes a little more planning. Where do you want to go? How do you plan to get there? Where can you stop along the way?

Take time to plan out your destination carefully before you grab your toothbrush. It might sound romantic to hop in your car and hit the road at a moment's notice, but it's not so romantic when you reach the highway and realize you have nowhere to go.

GET YOUR FACTS STRAIGHT There are more places than ever with a wealth of information about any destination you're considering. Check out what these sources have to say before you make your plans:

▶ Guidebooks: In addition to helping you with specifics once you arrive, guidebooks can ease your planning. They'll give you contact information, detailed maps, and sample itineraries.

▶ Web sites: The Internet offers thousands of pages devoted to different destinations. You'll find sites from travel professionals, media outlets, tourist boards, and fellow travelers at the click of a mouse.

▶ Travel agents: These professionals can facilitate your travel arrangements, since they know all the difficulties you might face on the way. Use their experience to your advantage, and listen to their advice.

▶ Tour operators: Here you'll find greater detail about the places you're planning to go. You'll get specific information to help you make exactly the right choices. Most brochures are free if you call to request them.

▶ Media: Check out your local newspaper's travel section, tune in to cable-television travel specials, or pick up a travel magazine for ideas on seasonal trips, hot destinations, or budget ideas.

▶ Friends and family: A travel guide can tell you what a destination has to offer in general, but your friends and family will be able to help you decide if a place is right for you. Arizona is lovely, but if you don't like the heat, it's not for you.

CHOOSING A DESTINATION

Picking where you want to go is the first step in planning a great road trip. There are many ways to think about destinations, and how you think will determine what kind of road trip you're going to have.

The most common kind of road trip has a single destination in mind. It might be a city like Chicago or a theme park like Walt Disney World, a single landmark like the Rock and Roll Hall of Fame or a certain spot in nature like the Grand Canyon. It could even be a favorite aunt's house. Whatever it is, this destination will shape your whole trip. You know exactly where you're starting from and ending up, so now you'll just need to figure out how best to get from Point A to Point B—and back from Point B to Point A. You'll also need to think about stopping at Point C along the way if your destination is far away.

Other trips have several stops along the way, each a destination unto itself. A trip to New England might

▶ **Great River Road:** Tracing the Mississippi River from its source in Minnesota to the Louisiana delta, this road—marked with signs emblazoned with steamboats—explores the heart of America.

▶ **Natchez Trace Parkway:** Following a pre-Columbian walking path, this road meanders from Natchez, Mississippi, to Nashville, Tennessee, passing Native American burial mounds, the ghost town of Rocky Springs, and Elvis's birthplace, in Tupelo, Mississippi.

▶ **Pacific Coast Highway:** Highway 101 runs from the beaches of southern California to the rugged forests of Washington's Olympic Peninsula.

▶ **Route 66:** If you know the song, you know that this American legend "winds from Chicago to L.A." Much of it has been made obsolete by interstates, but some of the old road and its rough-hewn roadside attractions survive thanks to a preservation movement. Signs denoting the historic route help keep you on track.

▶ **Skyline Drive:** Cutting through Virginia's Shenandoah Mountains, this route offers spectacular views and passes several natural underground caverns—a favorite for kids.

▶ **The Tamiami Trail:** Highway 41 extends from Miami on the Atlantic to Naples on the Gulf of Mexico, passing through the Everglades, Big Cypress National Preserve, and Ten Thousand Islands National Wildlife Refuge.

include a stop in Rhode Island to view the spectacular mansions in Newport, another stop in Boston to hear the symphony, and yet another stop in Acadia National Park in Maine to commune with nature before winding back through New Hampshire for some bargain hunting at the outlet stores. This kind of trip requires more thought, since each stop entails additional planning for lodging, dining, and sightseeing. But this is an ideal kind of trip for families with teenagers who get bored easily, and for anyone with at least a week to spend on the road.

Sometimes, the road itself is the attraction. In 2002, the U.S. Secretary of Transportation designated 13 new All-American Roads and 23 new National Scenic Byways—a collection of federally named "roads less traveled" that are considered national landmarks. It's quite a diverse list: Montana's Beartooth Scenic Byway and Louisiana's Creole Nature Trail joined the Acadia Byway in Maine and the Strip in Las Vegas on the list of All-American Roads. The list of National Scenic Byways, which already included such roads as Connecticut's Merritt Parkway and West Virginia's Coal Heritage Trail, now also includes Missouri's Little Dixie Highway and Alaska's Glenn Highway. These roads aren't just a way to get from Point A to Point B; they're the whole point of the trip.

One Place to Go

Pick up a road map and you'll see how many places you can go in every direction. Maybe you'll head for a small town, to sample fresh crabs in Crisfield,

CELEBRATED CITIES

► **Boston:** Walk the historic Freedom Trail, take a swan boat ride in Boston Public Garden, and grab a fantastic Italian dinner in the North End.

► **Chicago:** Take in a Cubs game, browse in the Magnificent Mile's swank shops, and take an architectural boat trip.

► **Las Vegas:** Check out the all-night casinos, get blinded by the neon on the Strip, and visit the latest theme hotels.

► **Los Angeles:** Hit the beach, stroll along the Hollywood Walk of Fame, meet Mickey Mouse at Disneyland, and keep an eye out for celebrities.

► **Miami:** Admire the South Beach's Deco District, perk up with a shot of coffee in Little Havana, learn to salsa at a fancy nightclub, and catch some rays on the city's sugar-sand beaches.

► **Montreal:** Practice your French in the cafés of the Quartier Latin, scale the heights of Mt. Royal, and enjoy the summer's outdoor jazz and comedy festivals.

► **New Orleans:** Soak up some jazz in the French Quarter, snack on beignets, experience Mardi Gras firsthand, and learn about voodoo's bewitching local history.

► **New York:** Taste an authentic bagel, see a Broadway show, take in the view from atop the Empire State Building, and splurge on a shopping spree.

► **San Francisco:** Climb aboard a cable car, drive across the Golden Gate Bridge, dine on dim sum in Chinatown, and relive your hippie days in the Haight.

► **Washington:** Head to the top of the Washington Monument, ponder great art at the National Gallery, and wander through colonial Georgetown.

Maryland, or shop for antiques in Grand Isle, Vermont. Perhaps you'll aim for a national park, like Yellowstone or Yosemite. Or maybe you've been dying to see a famous tourist attraction like Mt. Rushmore or Graceland. You might want to plunge into a favorite sport and choose to go skiing in Aspen or fishing in the Florida Keys. You might even take a road trip just to see a onetime event, like a sports game, rock concert, or state fair.

From New York to Los Angeles, big cities are a major draw. No matter how much hometown pride you've got, it's always a treat to see what life is like in another city. Great cities offer a vibrant pace, distinctive architecture, diverse culture, and incredible nightlife options. Whether you live in a big city or prefer a more rural life most of the year, check out a new city and you'll find enough to keep you entertained for quite a while. Cities are ideal for luxury travelers, since fancy hotels and top-notch restaurants beckon, but you can also visit most cities for less.

Beach trips are particularly popular for families, especially when school-age kids are on summer vacation. They're fun for all ages, casual, and relatively cheap. Depending on the beach, you might have a wide variety of things to do, from the usual swimming and splashing around to fishing, surfing, boating, snorkeling, and windsurfing. Choose your preferred level of diversion: Would you like to be near a lively boardwalk or oceanfront amusement park, or would you rather find a quiet stretch of sand?

UNBEATABLE BEACHES

On the Atlantic

▶ **York County coast, Maine:** U.S. 1 skirts a string of coastal towns, most notably Kennebunkport. All the classic elements are in place: sturdy clapboard houses, rocky shores, and lobster boats (not to mention ultrafresh lobster on local menus).

▶ **Cape Cod, Massachusetts:** Not far from breathtaking beaches are lovely New England villages full of shops and galleries to fill your days.

▶ **Nantucket and Martha's Vineyard, Massachusetts:** Off-season, these idyllic beaches feel miles away from the crowds and noise.

▶ **Atlantic City, New Jersey:** Besides the casinos that line the famous boardwalk, there are glitzy shows, great concerts, and non-stop nightlife.

▶ **Cape Hatteras, North Carolina:** The remote, uncrowded shores are perfect for watching wildlife or catching fish.

▶ **Hilton Head, South Carolina:** High-end resorts and condo complexes feature country-club amenities along the wide beach.

▶ **Palm Beach, Florida:** This community still bears the signs of its long history as a hideaway for the wealthy, in its ultraexclusive shopping and stately mansions.

On the Gulf

▶ **Naples, Florida:** Along soft white beaches, one of the state's fastest-growing cities is booming with shopping and fine arts—yet it's still just a short drive from the untouched natural wonders of the Everglades.

▶ **Mississippi Gulf Coast:** Try your luck at the casinos at Biloxi and Gulfport, or get away from the noise on an excursion to National Park beaches from nearby Ocean Springs.

▶ **South Padre Island, Texas:** Gentle Gulf waters lap at peaceful, wide beaches where seabirds gather.

On the Pacific

▶ **Monterey, California:** Trendy boutiques, galleries, and cafés beckon, and golfers can work on their handicaps at nearby courses.

▶ **Huntington Beach, California:** Surfers are drawn to this area's waves, while landlubbers can enjoy the lively pier.

▶ **Newport Beach, California:** One of California's upscale scenes, Newport is a haven for yachters.

▶ **La Jolla, California:** A gracious small town plus the caves and underwater preserve of La Jolla Cove add up to a winning combination.

▶ **Rosarito, Mexico:** Just across the border, you can go horseback riding on the beach during the day and later enjoy the lively nightlife in nearby Tijuana.

Perhaps the most common type of road trip, family visits are usually the least expensive, since lodging is often included at your relatives' house. Whether you're going to a family reunion or a wedding or just taking your kids to visit their grandparents, traveling to see relatives is something most people do regularly, during the holidays or whenever else they have the time.

Many Places to Go

Sometimes you won't be able to choose just one place to visit. Or perhaps there are several places you'd like to go in the same general vicinity, but you don't think any one of those places would justify a long trip on its own. A road trip is particularly well suited to this kind of travel; with air travel, you pay huge surcharges for anything other than a simple round-trip, point-to-point ticket, and with rail travel, you're limited to the places the trains go. But in a car, you can make as many stops as you want, on a route as circuitous as it needs to be.

Your trip might be fairly small in scope—touring the Finger Lakes in upstate New York, for instance. Or you might broaden it a bit, say, taking in the foliage across New England in autumn. Or you might make it the ultimate road trip: driving across the entire United States. Whatever you choose, you'll be able to make plans that suit exactly what you want to see for exactly the right amount of time. These are the times you'll truly appreciate the advantages of taking a road trip as opposed to other forms of transportation.

The Road as a Destination

Whether you've decided to check out some of this country's scenic byways or explore what's left of historic Route 66, you've got a bit of planning to do. You'll still need to find places to stop along the road—maybe even off the road—to eat and sleep. You'll also need to figure out how to get to the road in the first place, which will inevitably entail taking other roads that are a bit less scenic or historic.

Every notable road has places to stay along the way, or at least in nearby towns. Figure out exactly which attractions you're most interested in seeing—even on Route 66 you'll find some stretches less interesting than others—and try to stop or stay overnight near these.

Being Spontaneous

Some people have an easy time being spontaneous. Of course, they often don't have families or a lot of responsibilities. They can come close to throwing darts at a map and taking off with little warning, free spirits going on a trip for the sake of getting away, with the destination less important than the journey itself. They decide they want to take a road trip first, and only second do they choose where to go.

But anyone can travel this way with some effort. Clear the deck for a few days—no appointments, no plans. Find a place for your kids to stay if you want to leave them behind. Then whisk your spouse away for a romantic weekend escape at the last minute; the fact that it's a short drive to the Jersey shore instead of a flight to Tahiti won't matter as much as the spontaneity of it all. If you're taking your children, pack their bags for them and tell them you're taking them on a mystery trip. It'll make it more exciting for them if they're caught unaware when you pull into a Six Flags amusement park where they can ride roller-coasters all day.

Decide how many hours you're willing to drive. For a weekend getaway, you probably won't want to travel more than a few hours in each direction, but for a week you might be willing to drive two days each way. Translate your driving time into distance, figuring you can go a maximum of about 50 mi for each hour on an interstate and much less on smaller roads that go through towns or wind through rough terrain. Get a road atlas and draw a circle around your hometown, taking in everything that's within your possible driving radius. Then take a look and see what's in that circle. There are probably places you never thought about before that are in easy reach: cities you've never visited, small towns with romantic guest houses, beaches or mountain resorts, historical sites, and natural wonders.

A friend and I take off on a road trip every time we have a three-day weekend. We figure we can drive about 10 hours in a day if we switch off, which will get us about 500 mi in a car. We check the **TRAVEL LOG** road atlas for a city we haven't been to. If we went north to Boston last time, we'll go south to Atlanta this time. On Friday we grab a road map, pack a weekend bag, and hit the road by lunchtime; then have a full weekend in a new place before coming back Monday.

–William A., Washington, D.C.

FAMILY VISITS Visiting a family member seems like it requires little planning. But there are a few things to consider for this kind of trip:

▶ What activities will you plan? Your relatives may be your hosts, but they are not your entertainment directors. Don't simply show up without at least a partial itinerary, expecting them to plan your days.

▶ What else is nearby? Sure, it's nice to visit Grandma in Florida, but does your 14-year-old daughter really want to spend a solid week of her summer vacation in a retirement village? Knowing there's a beach a few minutes away will help make this family visit more fun for everyone.

▶ How long are you welcome? These visits are often stressful for the hosts. Grandpa might not be used to having little kids making a ruckus in his house, and your little cousins might not want to share their bedrooms with your kids for very long. Discuss this with your hosts in advance. As a rule, houseguests and fresh fish turn rotten after three days. Remember: You can still visit your relatives without staying in their homes. Look into a nearby hotel if you're planning a longer visit.

▶ Can you make this a vacation for everyone? Instead of driving to Uncle Jack's house and staying with him, drive to Uncle Jack's house, pick him up, and take the whole family to a different city. Your family will still get quality time together, but everyone will be able to enjoy a vacation.

CHOOSING A ROUTE

Before you ease on down the road, you've got to pick the right road. The route you choose will depend on your priorities: Are you trying to get to your destination as quickly as possible, or would you like to check out the places you're passing along the way? Do you like to take the scenic route or just the most direct one?

Interstates provide the quickest way to cover long distances in the United States. With limited access, few curves, and high speed limits, you can cruise along at a steady clip—assuming there's no traffic. Of course, that's a big "if." Often, interstates are heavily trafficked by truckers carrying loads between cities and local commuters in metropolitan areas. Just because the speed limit is 65 mph doesn't mean cars are always moving that quickly. Avoid rush hours near cities, and check road reports for construction or accidents that slow down the traffic. Even if you plan to take interstates exclusively, plan out alternate routes before you take off each morning, because you never know when you'll hit unexpected traffic jams and you'll want to change your plans.

According to a recent survey by the Federal Highway Authority, 76% of travelers prefer to take the most interesting route rather than the quickest. This often involves taking local highways and smaller roads that have traffic lights, fewer lanes, and lower speed limits. But a route like this is a great way to soak up local culture, stumble across attractions you didn't know about, and make your drive less monotonous.

Of course, you don't need to choose only one option. The best trips mix up the route to take advantage of the best features of each. Try taking the slow route when leaving home and the fast route when going home. Or take interstates between towns but exit onto local roads to get through those towns. Maybe you'd prefer to make good time on major roads early in the morning but look for a restaurant on a smaller road for a lunch break, rather than stop at a fast-food joint on I-95.

Keep in mind that many roads involve tolls, particularly over bridges. The fees are small, but they do add up; a trip from Washington, D.C., to Boston via New York might include $20 in tolls. That's not a fortune, but choosing alternate toll-free routes might save enough for you and your traveling companion to have dinner in Harvard Square.

Road Maps

There are many types of maps: fold-up maps, spiral-bound trip planners, laminated or plain paper, bound road atlases. Whichever kind you prefer, make sure to take along at least two. You'll need the largest-scale map to get from one city or state to another, but you'll also need smaller-scale local maps for the places you plan to explore; a fold-up map of the East Coast won't tell you how to get from your hotel in Baltimore's Inner Harbor to Camden Yard for an Orioles game. Make sure your maps are current by checking their copyright dates. Encountering roadwork of some degree is almost as reliable as death and taxes. Even if

GETTING MAPS

Where can you find a good road map?

▶ **Auto clubs:** Many auto clubs offer maps free to members. AAA's Trip Tiks are particularly useful, since they mark your planned route and come in an easy-to-handle, readable booklet.

▶ **Bookstores:** The travel section will likely have both bound map booklets and fold-up maps for popular destinations. If you're going to a major city, you can also find urban maps with street locators, so you can find side streets and exact addresses.

▶ **Gas stations:** In the old days, maps used to be available for free when you filled your tank. These days, the same, reliable fold-up maps are still available, but they'll cost you a couple of dollars. They're typically regional maps, best for finding major highways and interstates, and handy for finding alternate major roads if you hit traffic on your planned route.

▶ **On-line:** Free sites allow you to print out your exact route door-to-door, with precise directions written out. Since you can zoom in on a single neighborhood, these maps are ideal for finding small streets or navigating dense urban areas. However, they tend to have more errors than published maps, so you should cross-check them with another source.

▶ **Rest stops:** If you didn't get a map ahead of time, or if you've already got a regional map but want to pick up one that covers a smaller area, check here.

you're familiar with your route or destination, road changes or construction could throw you off course; having an up-to-date map can help you get back on track.

Plot out your planned route on your road map, using a highlighter to mark the roads you'll be taking. This will let you locate your route at a glance. Additionally, write out the route on a piece of paper, including exit numbers, distances, and directions. This will be easier to read quickly while you're driving. Just keep your highlighted road map handy in case you need to double-check your directions or change routes. Also, have a small flashlight on hand for reading the directions or map after dark.

Members of AAA may want to get one of the auto club's famous Trip Tiks for a road trip. These are custom-made to contain exactly the maps you'll need on your

My son and I decided to drive to Lake Onderdonk, where my family once had a cabin. I hadn't seen it for 50 years, so I was very excited about the trip. But once we were on the road, I **TRAVEL LOG** noticed the map I brought didn't even have this little lake on it. What should have been an hour-long drive ended up being two or three. I learned my lesson: Always bring more than one map.

–John S., Lakeland, Florida

trip, arranged in a spiral-bound, flip-top booklet so you'll never have to worry about folding and unfolding a large road map, or losing your place. Your planned route will be outlined on the Trip Tik, so it's easy to follow. You can pick up a Trip Tik in a AAA office or order one on-line.

There are also a variety of Internet sites that will plot out directions to your destination. All you need to do with on-line services such as Map Blast and Map Quest is enter your starting and ending points, and the program does the rest. They map out your route, giving detailed driving instructions. They also print out easy-to-follow maps. You can then print out all this information to take with you on your trip.

Just remember that even good technology can go bad. A recent survey of several on-line resources in the *Wall Street Journal* found that some gave misleading or mistaken directions. They also may not find the shortest route between two points, especially if it involves getting off the major roads. Not recommending a popular ferry, for example, took travelers several hours out of their way.

Some cars—including many rental cars—come equipped with onboard navigation systems. These global positioning systems can plan out your routes, tell you exactly where you are (even if you're lost), and advise you of alternate routes. They can even speak aloud so you won't have to take your eyes off the road. This kind of system is particularly useful if you're traveling alone and don't have someone to serve as a navigator.

However, it's not impossible for these systems to break down.

The solution? Bring traditional paper maps as a backup just in case you have technical difficulties.

Every time I take my boys on a road trip, I photocopy a map of the places we're going and laminate them at the copy shop. Then I use the laminated maps as place mats at dinner for several days before we leave. It gives

TRAVEL LOG the boys a chance to learn about our trip and see exactly where we're going to be driving. It always gets them excited.

–Tom D., New York, New York

Stopping Along the Way

If the place you're headed is more than several hours' drive away from home, you may need to stop along the way. First, decide how you want to divide up the drive: If you have a 10-hour journey, would you prefer to drive 8 hours the first day, so you'll arrive at your ultimate destination before lunchtime on the second day? Or would you rather split the driving more evenly?

Next, decide what you want to get out of this stop. Are you just looking for a place to spend a night and then want to get right back on the road in the morning? If so, you'll probably want to find accommodations that are as cheap as possible, as close to the road as possible, and outside a city. If you'd like to make your stop more of a mini-destination, find a town or city where you can sleep—even if it involves going a few miles off your direct course. That way, you can experience a few hours in a new place—find a good restaurant, see a movie, do some shopping—and you won't feel like you're simply "in-transit" to somewhere else. This requires a bit more planning, so you'll know exactly where you're going and where you're sleeping, and what it is you want to see during your brief stay.

On your ride home, you don't have to stop in the same place. If you are simply looking for a pit stop, pulling into a motel to grab a good night's sleep, it probably

When we drove up the California coast from Los Angeles to San Francisco, we took the old coastal road. It's slow and winding, but the views are spectacular, like nothing we'd ever seen. We split the drive up into two days, stopping in San Luis Obispo for the night and spending a whole morning in San Simeon. It made the ride up truly thrilling. On the way home, though, we just wanted to get back to L.A. as soon as possible, so we took the interstate inland. The drive was totally unremarkable, even ugly in some places, but it got us home quick—in one day with hours to spare.

TRAVEL LOG

–*Christopher H., West Hollywood, California*

doesn't matter. But if you are trying to see something new, savor a few minutes of excitement on the road, or keep your kids entertained, stop in a different place.

The Ride Back Home

Where is it written that you must return home on the same road you used to leave home? Coming back a different route can make your time on the road more interesting. You can plan your itinerary in a circle, where you never pass the same place twice—taking a northwestern route one way and a southeastern route back, for instance. Or you can take the same general route along different roads—taking a freeway in one direction but nearby side roads on the way back.

Sometimes you just want to get there and back as quickly as possible, and you don't care so much about what you pass along the way. But if you vary the roads you take, you can make your trip more interesting, and you could end up seeing twice as much as if you'd simply backtracked.

DIVIDING DRIVING DUTIES

The driver on a road trip is like the captain on a cruise ship. You're the one who decides where the car is going and when. But just as a captain has a first mate, the driver needs some assistance to handle the job.

A navigator is a must. On long journeys, you'll probably want an additional driver to switch off. And if you're traveling with kids, you'll want someone to supervise them—to break up arguments, read books aloud, or play games. These jobs aren't mutually exclusive. In fact, on a family trip, one parent usually drives while the other navigates, watches the children, and prepares to take the wheel at the next stop. Decide before you leave how you're going to divide driving duties, so everyone knows what's expected.

Drivers

If possible, make sure everyone who has a driver's license is prepared to share the driving duties. Switching off who's behind the wheel helps fight driver fatigue. Change places *before* the driver gets tired, though.

If you're renting a car and planning to have more than one driver, tell the rental agent when you pick up your car; have each driver provide a driver's license and credit card, and there may be a small additional fee per driver. It's best to sign up all potential drivers on a rental car, even if all of them don't plan on driving. You never know when a driver will get tired or need someone else to take the wheel.

Plan to take a break every two hours on the road—whether you think you need it or not. Even if it's just a few minutes to stretch your muscles, use a rest room, or get a drink of water, it'll help break up the trip. It's also a good chance to switch drivers. If you're traveling with children, you'll probably need to stop more frequently.

If you're driving alone, or if you're the only driver in the car, don't drive more than 8 to 10 hours in a single day. Plan to stop before you get tired—by that point, it's too late to start looking for a place to spend the night. Plan to stop each night by dinnertime if possible, so you can relax and get a good night's sleep before the next day's drive.

Navigators

Navigators are in charge of the maps and the route. They should keep the written route directions and all the highlighted maps on hand and in neat order. They can also handle toll payments and plan alternate routes in case of traffic jams or roadwork. In short, they're responsible for helping you stay on time and on track.

MAKING A GETAWAY

There are many ways to plan a trip, but you've always got to plan your destination first. Sometimes, it's obvious from the outset; if your kids are aching to see Walt Disney World, it's an easy decision. Other times you just need to get away, and you come up with a specific place to visit later.

Either way, choose your destination well. Make it a place that everyone on the trip will enjoy. And plan a route that satisfies your desires, whether they're primarily about speed or more focused on stopping to smell the flowers. Once you've got a place and a route set, your trip has a shape, a purpose, and a reason for being. Then you're ready to work on the details.

2

YOUR CHARIOT AWAITS

When you take a plane, you have to trek out to the airport, wait in long lines to check in, and then wait another hour or two before boarding, all the while crossing your fingers that your flight isn't delayed. Taking a road trip is much simpler. Chances are, your car is parked out front right now, ready for boarding. And if you want to change the schedule, it's all up to you. You are passenger and pilot rolled into one.

Of course, you're also the maintenance chief, so you've got to make sure your car is ready for the journey. Otherwise you might run into some unexpected turbulence down the road.

You also need to decide if you've got the appropriate vehicle for the trip. The car in your driveway may be convenient but it's not your only option. If it isn't the right vehicle for your trip—or if you don't have a car of your own—not to worry. Thanks to car rental companies, you have access to any kind of car you might need. You might not want to take a car at all—a motor home might be a cozier, cheaper option for a family, or a motorcycle might be more exciting if you're traveling alone. Start by thinking of who will be traveling, where you'll go, and how long the trip will be. A pause for reflection might lead you to an unexpected but better choice.

TAKING YOUR OWN CAR

Your own vehicle is convenient and familiar and gives you maximum flexibility, with freedom to drive as far as you want and bring it back whenever you're ready. And you don't have to worry about any additional costs beyond getting a tune-up and filling the gas tank.

But is it that simple? Is your car up to the drive? Are you willing to put your car through the wear and tear of a long trip?

YOUR OWN WHEELS OR OTHERS?

As you consider whether you want to use your own car or spring for a rental, weigh the following priorities:

▶ **Comfort:** Is your car really a place you'll enjoy spending several hours at a stretch? Is there enough room for everyone? Do the amenities, like the sound system, make the grade?

▶ **Economics:** If your own car isn't quite right, how much are you willing to spend to get something closer to your ideal? Figure in gas mileage; those fill-ups add up.

▶ **Practicality:** Can the vehicle tackle the physical demands of the trip you've planned? Will it offer enough room? Will you be able to maneuver it easily?

▶ **Speed:** How quickly do you need to get to your destination? A sports car moves more quickly than a motor home.

▶ **Style:** Do you want to make a statement on the road?

Time for a Tune-up

When's the last time you had your oil changed? Does it look like black gold or Texas tea? Do your windshield wipers smear or clear the glass?

The last place you want such little irritations to turn into major headaches is on the road, far from home. So take your car in for a checkup at least a few days before you leave, so that you can conveniently schedule any necessary repairs. At home, you may have a mechanic you trust or you can ask for recommendations. Once you're on the road, you have much less control over when and where to have repairs done.

In addition to addressing any problems you already know about, you should have your mechanic do a routine check of the following vital areas:

▶ Tire pressure: Proper air pressure lessens the wear on your tires. If you'll be driving in cold weather, remember that a tire can lose a pound or more of pressure for each drop of 10 degrees, which can impair the tire's traction on snow and ice. Don't forget to check the pressure in your spare tire.

▶ Oil: How long has it been since you had your oil changed? In addition to checking the level, you should have your oil changed every 3,000 mi. In summer, switch to the heavier grade needed to protect your engine during warm-weather driving. Check your owner's manual for information on the appropriate oil.

▶ Brakes: Squeaking could indicate a deeper problem, principally worn brake pads. If brake pads are left to deteriorate, they'll become ineffective. Make sure your brake pads have plenty of wear left in them.

▶ Windshield wipers and fluid: The National Highway Transportation Board recommends installing new wipers every year. If you'll be driving in freezing conditions, it's especially important to have a full container of fluid—and an extra gallon in your trunk.

▶ Air-conditioning fluid: If you have a leak, it's not only inconvenient, but it can also be bad for the environment, since Freon damages the ozone layer.

EMERGENCY SUPPLIES

- ☐ Spare keys
- ☐ Oil
- ☐ Wiper fluid
- ☐ Tire fixative
- ☐ Spare tire
- ☐ Jack
- ☐ Piece of light wood about 2 ft square
- ☐ Lug wrench
- ☐ Jumper cables
- ☐ Battery terminal cleaner
- ☐ Flashlight
- ☐ Safety flares
- ☐ Hand towel
- ☐ Bottle of water
- ☐ Tire block

In cold weather:

- ☐ Antifreeze
- ☐ Deicer spray and scraper
- ☐ Snow shovel
- ☐ Bag of sand

Preparing for the Unexpected

Just as you should pack a first-aid kit, you should prepare an automotive repair kit to equip you to handle the problems drivers often face. (For information on how to deal with car-related problems, see Chapter 5.)

Bring a spare set of car keys and keep them in your pocket at all times; getting locked out of your car can be a costly hassle. You'll need extra oil and wiper fluid; have a flashlight and safety flares on hand in case something goes wrong after dark. A jack, a lug wrench, a tire block, and a spare tire are the basic supplies for fixing a flat tire. A set of jumper cables will get your battery running again if it dies. In addition to a shovel, antifreeze, and deicers for cold-weather driving, you should consider snow tires or radials, too.

A couple of items that may not seem like car supplies will come in handy. A bottle of water can be a lifesaver if your radiator overheats. A piece of wood can provide a steady, flat surface for a jack. And an old hand towel or rag will help keep the interior of your car clean after you've changed a tire, added fluids, or checked anything under the hood.

Getting Your Papers in Order

In addition to your driver's license and registration, be sure you also take all of your insurance information and your membership card if you belong to an auto club. If you're going to be crossing international borders, you will need additional papers. Acceptable proofs of citizenship include passports, certified birth certificates presented with a government-issued photo identification, and naturalization certificates; note that drivers' licenses and Social Security cards do not count as proofs of citizenship. Make sure you have all the required documents—including those for children—before you take off, or you could jeopardize your trip.

HEADED TO CANADA? United States citizens entering Canada need proof of citizenship, preferably a passport. Citizens of all other countries require passports.

MEXICO BOUND? U.S. and Canadian citizens crossing into Mexico need proof of citizenship, while everyone else needs a passport. Once your citizenship has been verified, you'll receive a free tourist card that allows you to stay in the country for up to 90 days. Don't lose it, as you need it to leave the country.

Mexico has particularly strict regulations about children crossing the border: All children under 18 must have proof of citizenship, and all minors traveling with a single parent must have a notarized letter from the other parent granting permission to cross the border. (If the other parent is deceased, or the child has only one legal parent, a notarized statement saying so must be presented as proof at the border.) If you're taking someone else's child to Mexico, you'll need a notarized letter of permission from the parents.

RENTING A CAR

If you don't own a car, renting might be your only option short of asking Dad to borrow the keys. But even if you've already got a car, renting might make sense.

Why rent a car, you may wonder, when you've got a perfectly good one in your driveway? There are plenty of solid, practical reasons as well as a few less utilitarian but equally valid incentives for leaving your own wheels at home. Don't feel restricted by the car you drive every day; you're better off getting the right vehicle for the trip than being uncomfortable.

If money is your main concern, remember that a rental car is much cheaper than most trips by plane or train. Also, renting saves wear and tear on your own car, and in the end, that saves you cash.

DOCUMENTS YOU'LL NEED When you rent a car, bring driver's licenses for all drivers and a credit card. You might also need to show proof of insurance, especially if you plan to decline the agency's insurance.

RESTRICTIONS FOR YOUNG DRIVERS Drivers under 25 face extra restrictions when renting cars. Some agencies don't rent to under-25 drivers at all. Some agencies rent to drivers under 25—but over 21—for an additional fee ranging from $5 to $25 per day. A few allow drivers as young as 18 to get behind the wheel, for an additional charge, as long as they have a credit card. Policies on underage drivers vary from company to company, and even from location to location within the same company. Beyond the rental rates, insurance rates on rental cars also go up for younger drivers. When you're calling to make a reservation, be sure to mention if any drivers are under 25, and ask if this is permitted and what any extra charges might be.

Size Matters

The best reason to choose a rental over your own car is space. There's no way you're going to fit six people in the backseat of your Volkswagen Beetle—unless you're traveling with circus clowns. And there's simply no room in your hatchback for a dozen suitcases.

You need to be sure you can fit everyone in the car and still have room for luggage. If you can't picture how you'll squeeze everything into the trunk, you probably won't be able to. Save yourself the cramped elbows and crumpled garment bags and rent a car that has the space you need. And don't be afraid to think big: Most agencies rent vans, which can be ideal for two families traveling together or for a group outing that requires bulky equipment.

WHAT CAR CATEGORIES MEAN You know what a convertible looks like, and you know what a van looks like, but what's the difference between a mid-size and full-size car? When you call to reserve a rental car, you'll be asked what size you want. These categories vary slightly from company to company, but here's a general idea of what they mean, from least expensive to most expensive:

▶ Economy: A subcompact car, often a two-door model, that seats four. Trunk space is extremely tight and the ride can be less than smooth. Examples: Chevrolet Geo Metro, Hyundai Accent.

▶ Compact: A small sedan that seats four or five. The trunk holds a few medium-size bags. Examples: Dodge Neon, Ford Escort.

▶ Mid-size: A sedan that seats five, with trunk space for several small bags or a couple of large suitcases. Examples: Pontiac Grand Am, Dodge Stratus.

▶ Full-size: A larger car that seats five comfortably, with a roomy trunk that holds several large suitcases. Examples: Ford Taurus, Dodge Intrepid.

▶ Premium: Similar in size to full-size, but with more options and a more luxurious interior. Examples: Buick LeSabre, Chrysler Concorde.

▶ Luxury: Seats six, with an extralarge trunk. Add-ons usually include a high-end sound system, leather upholstery, and individual climate control. Examples: Lincoln Town Car, Cadillac DeVille.

There were four of us traveling, so we rented a mid-size car for the weekend. But our local agency considered a Nissan Sentra to be a mid-size car—it didn't have enough trunk space for all of us. We had to upgrade and pay extra at the last minute. **TRAVEL LOG** Now I always ask exactly what model I'll be getting.

–Stephen C., Brooklyn, New York

Weighing the Options

Maybe you're not the type who cares much about luxury add-ons when you're buying a car. But on a road trip, you could be essentially living in that automobile for much of the day. Options that seem like luxuries for your daily 15-minute commute might seem like necessities on a 15-hour drive on an interstate.

If you're headed someplace hot, powerful air-conditioning will make your days much more bearable. A good stereo can help the hours pass more quickly; you may want to rent a car with a tape deck or CD-player, especially for those parts of the country where you can't pick up anything but a few fuzzy AM stations on the radio. You may wish to go for a car with a satellite radio system, which guarantees a good choice of clear, reliable programming no matter where you are in the country. Both the XM and Sirius radio providers broadcast a variety of music and talk radio; XM includes advertising on some channels but Sirius is ad-free. Car rental companies are gradually adding these systems to their roster of options. And if you've ever wondered what cruise control is for, a long stretch of smooth, straight pavement will answer your question; now's your chance to give it a try. Renting is an easy way to take advantage of extras without paying to have them installed in your own car.

While you probably don't need a satellite navigation system to find your way to the grocery store at home, a device like OnStar can come in handy if you're traveling somewhere unfamiliar—especially if you're alone.

Many rental agencies offer these systems on their vehicles; this alone might justify leaving your car at home and renting one instead.

If you're a nonsmoker, request a smoke-free car.

Traveling in Style

A road trip can present an opportunity for you to change your image—just for a few days. Renting a car for reasons of style can change the whole tone of your road trip. Suppose you and your spouse have planned a weekend getaway to the beach, leaving your kids behind at Grandma's; will you *really* feel footloose and fancy free driving off in the minivan you use to carpool to soccer practice? Imagine the same trip in a rented convertible: It's romantic and somewhat decadent, and it'll definitely feel more like a vacation.

Sometimes, style pairs with substance. No matter how cute your sporty coupe might be, you're better off get-

---

TRAVEL LOG

When we headed down the Florida coast in March, we went to the rent-a-car agency to pick up the compact we'd reserved. When we got to the lot, we noticed they were having a special on convertibles. We splurged and went with the convertible. It was only $10 a day more, but it made our spring break a time we'll never forget.

–William C., Columbia, South Carolina

---

ting a four-wheel-drive vehicle to trek through the Rockies in winter. Think about what style of car is appropriate for your trip, and if the car you own doesn't fit the image, rent one that does.

Specialty Vehicles

In addition to renting sedans, most rental agencies offer "specialty vehicles" in a variety of shapes and sizes. If you're traveling alone or with one other person, you can reserve a smaller car—a convertible or sports car—with only two seats. If you don't need the extra seats and trunk space, this is a great way to jazz up your trip.

You've also got options if a traditional car doesn't seem big enough or doesn't seem quite right for the trip. Most rental companies have fleets of minivans for family travel, full-size vans for larger groups, and SUVs for people traveling over rougher terrain requiring four-wheel-drive.

Reckoning the Cost

When you're calculating the cost of a rental vehicle, remember to price the extras:

▶ Collision- or loss-damage waiver: Always optional, it should never be automatically added to your bill. It runs as high as $20 per day, and it's a good idea if your own car insurance doesn't cover you for rentals.

▶ Bodily injury damage: This protection against injuring other drivers is optional but a good idea if your own insurance doesn't cover you.

▶ Mileage charge: Sometimes a few cents per mile are added after you exceed a daily or weekly mileage maximum included in the base rental rate.

▶ Refueling charge: To avoid this, fill up the car yourself before returning it. Or you could choose a pre-pay option: The rental company will refill the tank for less than the standard drop-off refueling fee.

▶ One-way services and drop-off charges: If you won't need the car once you arrive, it might be cheaper to reserve two one-way trips, even with the added drop-off fees, than to reserve a car for a whole week and let it sit idle for five days at your destination.

▶ Local and state taxes.

▶ Child seats.

▶ Additional service fees.

SAVING MONEY Most rental agencies offer discounts to members of their premium clubs; if you plan to rent cars often, it might be worth paying the annual membership fee to receive these discounts. Many car rental agencies also offer a variety of special discounts, open to nonmembers. Be sure to check if any of the following apply to you:

▶ Weekend fares: If you're flexible, you can often save by renting on a weekend instead of a weekday.

▶ Special promotions: A large sedan might actually be cheaper than an economy car during a special promotion. Discounts on weekly rentals might actually make a seven-day rate cheaper than a five-day rate, even if you only need the car for five days. Be sure to ask.

▶ Internet rates: Surfing the Web might help you find an otherwise unadvertised rate.

▶ Community organizations: Many clubs and organizations, such as AAA and AARP, receive special rates.

▶ Age discounts: Senior citizens may be eligible for lower fares.

▶ Credit cards: Some credit card companies offer discounts if you charge your rental on their plate.

▶ Frequent flyers: Many airline programs offer lower rates on car rentals at participating agencies; you might earn frequent flyer miles without leaving the ground.

▶ Government, military, and corporate rates: Sometimes cheaper fees apply with proper identification.

OPTING FOR AN RV

Traveling in a motor home, or recreational vehicle (RV), can give your road trip a whole different flavor. RV enthusiasts say the vehicles are conducive to more intimate family vacations while at the same time offering great flexibility when planning.

Motor homes are especially popular with families. A study conducted by polling firm Louis Harris and Associates found that 92% of parents who own an RV said that they are the best way to travel with family and children, and 63% of parents who have never owned an RV agreed.

RV ownership has reached record levels; according to a 2001 survey commissioned by the Recreational Vehicle Industry Association, there are more than 7 million RVs on the road in the United States. If you don't own an RV, renting is a great way to enjoy the benefits of one of these family-friendly vehicles without making a major investment. You don't need a special permit to drive an RV; a standard driver's license will do.

The Advantages

Comfort is the most obvious advantage that a motor home has over a car. There's more room to spread out and move around. If you're sleepy, you can nap in an actual bed, rather than recline in a car's bucket seat. If you want a snack, you can sit at a table instead of getting crumbs all over yourself as you balance a plate on your lap.

An RV is also more convenient than a car in several ways. Tired of stopping at every other rest stop to use a bathroom—one that might not be as clean as you'd prefer? Your RV probably has a bathroom on board, so there's no need to stop. Desperate for a hot meal but wary of visiting another roadside burger joint? Most RVs have a kitchen, so you can make your own meals. Worried about finding a motel where you can stop for the night? Your bed is ready when you are.

W e were dreading another long drive to Grandma's house with all three kids crammed in the backseat. They were teenagers already, and there just wasn't enough room. My husband and I

TRAVEL LOG decided to rent a motor home, and it made all the difference. We didn't have any arguments the whole trip. Plus my son got to sleep in a bed that folded up into the ceiling at night, which he thought was really cool.

–Donna P., Bolingbrook, Illinois

If you're heading to the wilderness for a nature trek, taking an RV also has a lot to recommend it over taking a car and sleeping in a tent. Your family will appreciate the creature comforts—especially if you're traveling with senior citizens or young children. You'll also feel safer knowing that you won't have to tiptoe into the woods if nature calls.

The biggest advantage working for RVs is economic. On average, studies show that RV vacations cost just half of a comparable trip using the family car and staying in motels. Compared to buses, trains, or planes, RVs offer savings up to 70% when food and accommodations are factored in.

The Disadvantages

A motor home isn't the right vehicle for every road trip. Rentals aren't cut out for weekend getaways, for instance, since the major companies generally have at least a three-day minimum rental period. Rental companies also have a few restrictions on where you can take a rig; for instance, Death Valley in summer is not the time or place for an RV.

If you're planning on staying at Aunt Betsy's house for free, then the bed in your RV doesn't represent a savings. If you're going solo, having all that extra room isn't particularly relevant. If an RV's benefits aren't pertinent for you, you're better off renting a car; it will cost you less, and you'll save on gas, too.

If you're looking forward to speeding down the highway, watching the world whip by, an RV isn't right for you, either. With its added size and weight, a motor home tops out at moderate speeds on the road. Also, while motor homes help you save on food and lodging, they cost you at the filling station; RVs typically get gas mileage around 8 to 10 miles per gallon—a fraction of that of most cars.

Consider where you'll be driving and stopping. A motor home might be perfect for a trip to the Grand Canyon, but its size and turning radius may well be a handicap on city streets.

You'll also need to stick to a tight pick-up and drop-off schedule. The major rental companies have specific time frames for both pickups and returns, sometimes as narrow as a couple of hours.

RV Wrangling

If you're a first-timer or if you haven't driven a certain RV model before, be sure to spend enough time familiarizing yourself with the vehicle and its equipment before you head out on the road. Rental agents will review the RV with you, and you should go through a dry run of operating the water heater, toilet, sewage hookup, and so forth. Try out the driver's seat and adjust the rearview mirrors as needed. Take a short test drive to note the rig's turning radius and the length of time it takes to brake and accelerate. Also practice backing up—always a two-person undertaking, with a passenger getting out and helping to guide the driver. The spotter must be visible in the rearview mirror at all times. Establish a couple of basic hand signals that the spotter can use to communicate, such as one hand held palm out while the other beckons backward to indicate "reverse slowly." Remember, in the words of one RV company executive, "You need to take along a sense of humor the first time you rent."

CONSIDERING RV FEATURES If you're renting a motor home, make sure the vehicle meets your needs before you choose a model:

▶ Sleeping arrangements: Is there enough space? Enough privacy? Are the beds big enough, and comfortable enough?

▶ Bathroom facilities: Is there a hot water heater sufficient to take a hot shower on board?

▶ Climate control: Is there adequate air-conditioning and/or heating for the whole unit, even when it's not in motion?

▶ Kitchen setup: Does it have the equipment you need? Microwave? Freezer? Dry storage space? Adequate fresh-water storage?

▶ Electrical source: Is there an electrical generator to meet your needs? Many campgrounds have electrical outlets, but if you're planning to go somewhere more isolated, you'll need to be self-sufficient.

▶ Automotive features: Does your RV come with cruise control? Also consider extras like TV/VCRs and stereos to keep your passengers entertained.

WHERE TO PARK IT Of the 16,000 campgrounds around the United States catering to RVs, half are privately owned commercial campgrounds. Some of these are simple facilities, but others resemble luxury resorts with swimming pools, golf courses, health spas, and other high-end amenities. These private sites are commonly found near popular travel destinations and near metropolitan areas. Publicly owned campgrounds are operated by governmental agencies in state and national parks, national forests and wildlife refuges, and other public lands. Public or private, most (but not all) campgrounds provide a few basics for visitors, including washrooms, dining and/or picnic areas, and hookups for electricity and water. Some RV travelers rely on highway rest areas for overnight parking spots. The parking lots of large shopping centers are also sometimes used as makeshift bases, but some post NO OVERNIGHT signs to deter freebie campers.

BEST OF BOTH WORLDS If you like the idea of having the comforts of home on the road but don't think a motor home is for you, consider a towable trailer. You can hitch a trailer to your car, truck, or SUV and achieve many of the benefits of a self-propelled motor home, including kitchen and bathroom facilities. Trailers are cheaper to buy or rent than their larger counterparts. They're more versatile, too: You can detach the trailer when you reach your stopping point, and use your car for short excursions.

TAKING A MOTORCYCLE

Some people ride motorcycles at every opportunity, believing that the only way to experience the road is to ride it on two wheels. If you're not one of them, a road trip might be your perfect excuse to try a long-distance motorcycle ride, provided you've had some experience and have the proper instruction and equipment. You can arrange for riding lessons through the Motorcycle Safety Foundation. There are motorcycle rental companies around the country where you can check out what model is right for you.

The Pros and Cons

If you don't like motorcycles, you probably won't be easily won over listening to testimonials touting the exhilarating feeling of freedom as you sail down the highway. But it's true: No other mode of transportation puts you in such close contact with your surroundings.

Beyond the psychological aspects, there are practical advantages to motorcycles. They're nimble on the road, easy to maneuver on freeways and city streets, and a cinch to park wherever you are. When it comes to gas mileage, they leave cars waiting at the pump.

It's hard to take your kids along on a motorcycle and it's also hard to carry much baggage. Whether these points are a plus or a minus depends on your perspective.

What's undeniable is that motorcycles are far more susceptible to the weather than cars or RVs; if you're driving in the rain, you're going to get very wet, and if you're driving in cool weather, you're going to get very cold.

There's also the safety factor. Accidents happen. Even if you're an excellent cyclist, you can still fall victim to the reckless driving of other motorists, and there's always the unexpected. In an accident a bike offers much less protection than a car.

What to Ride

For a relatively modest trip, look for a bike with a cruiser design, saddlebags, and an engine of at least 650 cc's. For long rides, aim for a sport/touring model with an engine of at least 800 cc's.

Motorcycle Necessities

Unlike renting a car, you can't just walk into a motorcycle rental company with a charge card and ride out a few minutes later. There are a few things you'll need:

▶ License: You need a special driver's license to operate a motorcycle. Check with your department of motor vehicles or the Motorcycle Safety Foundation for information on how to obtain this permit.

▶ Helmet: Laws regarding helmet use vary from state to state, some requiring all riders to wear them, others requiring only young riders to do so, and a few not requiring them at all. Be sure to find out about helmet laws in all states you plan to visit. Even if it's not mandatory, wearing a helmet will reduce your risk of injury, so it's always wise to wear one. Bring an extra helmet in case you want to give a friend a ride.

▶ Gear: Like any other sport, motorcycle touring has specialized clothing and gear. Leather riding gloves are a must, as are boots with nonskid soles and long pants—preferably jeans, leather pants, or something similarly sturdy. Earplugs can save your hearing as the wind rushes by at 60 mph. Bring long johns, a thick scarf, and, for wet weather, a rain suit. You could also spring for posh items like heated gloves and helmets with two-way radios.

MAKING THE RIGHT CHOICE

There's a lot to consider when choosing a vehicle for your road trip. Remember that some of these choices require advance planning. The car you want to rent might not be available on the spur of the moment, and certainly not at the price you want to pay. Taking an RV might necessitate more research into campgrounds, which might require reservations. Choosing a motorcycle might mean lining up a refresher training course.

But once you've made your choice, you're ready to take a breath and think about how you're going to get everything you want to take inside.

3

IT'S IN THE BAG

So you know where you're going, and you know how you're going to get there. Seems like the tough part of planning your road trip is behind you, right?

Don't start jangling those car keys just yet—you haven't tackled one of the most important parts of your trip. Part science, part art, packing can make all the difference in how your journey goes. Plan well and you won't give it another thought for the rest of your trip. Plan poorly and you'll find yourself thinking about packing constantly while you're away: "I really should have packed the blow dryer." "That duffel bag made my good shirt look like I slept in it." "What's in this suitcase, a guilty conscience?"

You can change routes if you hit traffic, switch radio stations if you don't like what you hear, or buy a burger if you get hungry en route. But it's not as easy or cheap to solve a packing oversight once you've left home. It's worth taking time to plan out exactly what you want to bring and how you want to pack it. You'll save yourself endless irritation down the road.

CHOOSING LUGGAGE

Picking the right bag isn't as simple as it sounds. Your favorite backpack is no good if it won't hold everything you need. That giant valise your grandmother gave you might hold everything, but that's not important if the bag won't fit in your car or if you can't lift it when it's full. A few small bags might seem easier to manage, but you don't want to be juggling them or have difficulty keeping track of where you've put certain things.

Remember those old television advertisements that had gorillas jumping up and down on suitcases to prove the bags' sturdiness? Today, most people are more concerned about being able to carry their bags comfortably than about fending off attacks by hyperactive primates. If you've got an old suitcase in your closet whose greatest selling point is that it could withstand monkey-thrashing, you might want to consider a bag with more practical advantages.

Do an inventory of your luggage and start thinking about what would be most appropriate for your trip. Don't be limited by what you already own; a new bag could make a significant difference in your travels. Chances are you'll use it on future trips as well. The right luggage is a good investment.

Suitcases

The longtime mainstay of luggage, the pullman suitcase—rectangular, with a hinged lid and centered handle—is still considered standard equipment for most travelers. It's the type of bag you'll most likely use by default, unless you have a specific reason to choose a different kind.

Pullmans are versatile, quite sturdy, and reasonably lightweight. The hard-sided pullmans are lighter than they used to be and are preferable if you're carrying anything fragile. Soft-sided pullmans, meanwhile, are increasingly durable; their flexible material makes

CHOOSING THE RIGHT BAG

Ask yourself a few key questions about the luggage you'd like to bring:

☐ Will it all fit in your vehicle?

☐ Will it keep your clothes neat?

☐ Will it protect any fragile items?

☐ Will it be light enough to carry?

☐ Will everything fit inside?

them a better candidate if you anticipate a tight squeeze in your trunk. Pullmans with wheels and a telescoping handle are nearly ubiquitous. Although your road trip may entail less time hauling luggage than if you were traveling by plane or train, having a wheeled suitcase may still be a good idea if you'll be unloading and moving your bags frequently. They can be a godsend when your hotel room is at the far end of a long hallway. Pullmans also give you the widest array of options, such as side pockets, built-in garment bags, and so on.

Garment Bags

If you're bringing fancy clothes, a garment bag is the best way to ensure that they'll survive the trip without major wrinkles or damage. No bag is perfect, though, so bring a small can of anti-wrinkle spray to freshen your formal clothes quickly, and pack a travel iron for more—pardon the pun—pressing needs.

If you've got spare room inside the passenger compartment, you can hang your garment bag from the hooks or bars over the windows in the backseat. This will allow your clothes to hang unfolded, much as they would in your own closet, keeping creases to a minimum. If space is scarce inside the vehicle, lay the garment bag flat on top of the other bags in the trunk. If need be, fold the garment bag into halves or thirds before laying it on top of the stack.

Duffel Bags

For flexibility, nothing beats a duffel bag. Soft-sided and frameless, duffels come in a variety of shapes and sizes, but they're all easy to pack—easy to overstuff, too, if you need to cram in one more thing. They can be pushed and squeezed into a trunk like Silly Putty. If you're traveling with casual clothing like T-shirts and jeans that don't need to be handled with care, a duffel bag is a convenient, inexpensive option.

Basic canvas duffels have one compartment, often with a single opening and a single strap. They're easy to sling over your shoulder and can accommodate a lot of clothing in a compact space. Fancier models have additional pockets, multiple zippers, handle straps, and even wheels; they are also made from other materials, like lightweight nylon or waterproof fabrics.

Backpacks

Intrepid travelers know that backpacks aren't just for camping anymore. Durable and easy to carry, backpacks are particularly suitable if you're going on an informal trip or a rugged vacation.

Backpacks perform similarly to soft-sided suitcases when it comes to your car trunk: they can handle a certain amount of squashing and still keep your belongings in place. Many backpacks have a lightweight internal frame; you'll sacrifice some flexibility, but that structure generally keeps your things in neater condition than they would be in a duffel. With two large back straps and, on larger models, waist straps, backpacks are easier to carry than duffels, too. But they're still lighter than most suitcases, and they leave your hands free. Some backpacks have wheels (covered by a zippered panel) and a handle so that they can be converted into a pullman.

Of course, if you're going camping, a backpack is virtually essential, especially if you're parking a long distance from where you're setting up camp. Larger backpacks can accommodate a rolled-up sleeping bag or other camping supplies. Many models have a detachable knapsack that you can use as a day pack.

Trunks

You may associate steamer trunks and foot lockers with classic Barbara Stanwyck movies, the stories of immigrants sailing to America, or your childhood sleepaway camp, but you probably don't think about using one anymore. There are, however, valid reasons for considering one for a road trip.

Granted, trunks are large, heavy, inflexible, and difficult to maneuver in a small car's storage area. Some of those very characteristics can be counted as advantages, though: their size and sturdiness will keep your clothes more orderly than most suitcases. They protect breakables and they cost a small fraction of most durable luggage. If your car can accommodate a trunk and your trip won't involve moving your things frequently or for long distances, a trunk can be a practical, economical choice.

At first I laughed when my husband suggested getting our trunk out of the basement. But it turned out to be handy on our camping trip. It kept our clothes dry when we were staying outside, and we

TRAVEL LOG could sit on it—or even use it as a table—during our trip. It was like a suitcase and a piece of furniture in one.

–Deborah E., St. Paul, Minnesota

GET PACKING

Now that you've chosen the perfect bag for your trip, you've got to fill it. Plan out what you need to bring carefully. You don't want to reach the woods only to find that you've left your hiking boots at home, or start dressing for an elegant dinner only to realize that you've forgotten the pumps that match your cocktail dress.

An equally troublesome and perhaps even more common problem is overpacking. Rather than trying to be prepared for any occasion, think pragmatically about the situations you're most likely to encounter.

Tailor Your Threads

Clothes make up the bulk of your luggage. You'll need to tailor both the amount and type of clothing to the trip you're taking. Write up a list of your planned itinerary, and then next to each item, plan an outfit. A sample day might look like this:

Breakfast with your kids: Jeans, T-shirt, green sweater, sneakers

Swimming in the hotel pool: Bikini, flip-flops

Lunch with clients: Gray skirt, print blouse, navy blue pumps

Afternoon drive: Sundress, white sandals

Dinner at Grandma's house: Khakis, white blouse, blue V-neck sweater, brown loafers

Night out dancing: Black skirt, turquoise shell, black pumps

Now go over your list and see what you can consolidate to save space. Think conservatively: One sweater might suffice instead of two. Skip the sundress and make jeans and a T-shirt your sole casual outfit. Pick a pair of shoes that you can wear to lunch and also to go dancing.

If you're embarking on a less-structured trip, use other points for planning. Weigh probable activities, the length of your trip, and the weather on your route and in your final destination. The more spontaneous your trip, the more important the multipurpose element becomes.

Instead of trying to pack for every possible fashion need, bring your most versatile clothes. A pair of leather low-heeled shoes might go with several outfits a woman is bringing. A plaid button-down shirt could be casual enough for a man to wear with jeans but still dressy enough to pass muster in a romantic restaurant. A loose blouse can be classy enough to wear to the theater but informal enough to wear open over a tank top for a starlit walk on the beach. Bring clothes that can be worn in multiple ways.

And while you're at it, think about color. It's a good idea to choose items that all look good together. That way you can mix and match items, expanding your outfit options. Leave out anything that can't be worn with several different things. "Statement" pieces often have only one thing to say.

Accessories can aid and abet versatile dressing, but be sure to choose items that don't take up too much room.

TRAVEL LOG

Whenever I go away, I take my most flexible clothes. Instead of bringing blue jeans for casual use and black pants for more formal occasions, I bring a pair of black jeans. Instead of bringing brown hiking boots and black shoes, I bring one pair of black boots—which look like black shoes under my black jeans. And the shirts I bring are all flexible enough for a nice restaurant or informal enough for a smoky bar. That way I don't have to change clothes every few hours.

—Zev A., Somerville, Massachusetts

Jewelry or a scarf that folds to a whisper's thinness is a good pick. Shoes and hats, on the other hand, eat up a lot of space and generally can't be compacted.

If you're going somewhere cold, bring multiple layers rather than a few bulky, heavy items. Then you can add or subtract layers as the temperature changes.

As for staples like socks, underwear, and T-shirts, bring a set for each day, and also pack enough for an extra day or two. You never know when you'll want to change out of a sweaty T-shirt or throw out a sock

PLANNING YOUR WARDROBE

There are several things to keep in mind when you're planning which clothes to pack:

► **Time:** How long will you be gone? Will you be doing laundry on the trip? Will you need one outfit per day, or more than one?

► **Style:** Will you need formal attire or casual? Both? You'll want modest clothes if you're visiting religious sites or conservative areas. If you're planning an outdoorsy trip, you'll want clothes you don't mind getting dirty.

► **Weather:** Will you need clothes for warm weather or cold? Remember that even in summer, long sleeves and long pants can be necessary in air-conditioned buildings.

► **Sports:** Will you need to bring special athletic gear? A swimsuit for the hotel pool? Workout clothes for a morning jog? Hiking boots?

with a hole in the toe. It's also best to be on the safe side in case you get held up a day or two longer than you planned on the road—because of traffic problems, car trouble, or a last-minute extension of your dream vacation.

AIRING YOUR DIRTY LAUNDRY If you'll be traveling for a long period of time, you may have to do laundry on the road. Plan which day you'll take time out to do laundry. It might not be possible *exactly* halfway through a trip, depending on where you are that day, so bring enough clothing to last a day or two past when you think you'll do laundry, and don't wait until the day you're out of underwear to look for a Laundromat. Even if you're only traveling for a few days, it's a good idea to bring a small bottle of detergent or Woolite. You'll be happy you brought it if you stain an item of clothing during your trip and need to remove it quickly, or if you run out of clothes a day earlier than you'd anticipated and need to wash a few things in your sink. If you're pressed for time, look for a Laundromat that will do your washing for you; you can spend a few hours sightseeing or having a meal, then come back and pick up your laundry.

Toiletries

Make a list of your toiletries. Don't assume that the place you'll stay will have everything you need or the brands you prefer. Travel-size containers are a great space saver in a small kit. Pack everything that might spill or break inside a resealable plastic bag, just in case. If you're not traveling alone you can save space and

TOILETRIES CHECKLIST

The last thing you want to do on your road trip is search for Q-Tips in a strange town. Here's a checklist for items you might want to include:

☐ Soap

☐ Toothbrush and toothpaste

☐ Dental floss

☐ Shampoo/conditioner

☐ Brush and comb

☐ Hair-care products

☐ Contact lenses and solution

☐ Deodorant

☐ Razor

☐ Shaving cream

☐ Facial cleansers

☐ Makeup

☐ Moisturizer and hand lotion

☐ Feminine supplies

☐ Birth control

☐ Cotton swabs

☐ Tissues

☐ Mouthwash

☐ Nail clippers and emery boards

☐ Tweezers

☐ Sunscreen

☐ Insect repellent

money by avoiding duplication: Bring one each of the basics (shampoo, toothpaste, etc.) for everyone to share.

The Little Extras

Make a list of all the other nonclothing items you'll need to bring. Put a first-aid kit at the top of your list; for details on what this should include, see Chapter 5. Small appliances like hair dryers, alarm clocks, cell phone rechargers and hands-free attachments, cameras, and travel irons are easy to forget. Will you need a portable crib or collapsible stroller for your little one? Will you need to bring gifts to people you're visiting? You should also bring along items you'll need for entertainment—not just for the driving time itself (see Chapter 4) but for the overnight stops. Paperback novels or playing cards are good, compact options. Pack extra film and batteries—they'll still be good if you don't use them on this trip. And don't forget a collapsible umbrella.

ADDITIONAL BAGS Throw a couple of large, resealable plastic bags in your luggage. They're perfect for bringing home wet clothes or small items, like jewelry or souvenirs, which might get lost in your suitcase. Also consider bringing a smaller day pack or tote bag. You can pack it inside a larger bag and bring it out as needed during the trip. Or it could double as an overnight bag—if you're taking a long trip that involves spending one or two nights on the road before you reach your final destination, fill the small bag with your toiletry kit and a change of clothes. That way, you

IN CASE OF EMERGENCY

A few supplies that can get you through life's little emergencies:

- ☐ Bottle/can opener/corkscrew
- ☐ Eyeglass repair kit
- ☐ First-aid kit
- ☐ Matches
- ☐ Sewing kit
- ☐ Sink stopper
- ☐ Swiss army knife
- ☐ Tweezers
- ☐ Wipes

won't have to disturb your monster suitcase at every stop along the way.

How to Pack

After you've made your list of exactly what you plan to bring, do laundry at least one day before you leave to make sure everything is clean. Iron anything that needs pressing. Fold everything neatly, and start making piles. Count off your socks, underwear, and T-shirts and stack them up. Then go through the outfits you planned earlier, and lay out all your clothing on your bed. Take one more look at your clothes and remove anything that's not absolutely essential, crossing deleted items off your list.

Pick out the clothes you plan to wear on your first day's drive, and set this outfit aside. This outfit should be comfortable above all else, something casual that you won't mind getting a little rumpled in the car. Dress in layers to accommodate hot afternoons and cool evenings; cardigans or zip-front sweatshirts work well since they're not cumbersome and you can take them off while driving. Wear something that can roll with the punches—a silk twinset likely won't stand up to changing a tire.

Next, separate your clothes according to which bag you're going to pack them in, if you're bringing multiple bags. Set aside your formal clothes for your garment bag, and casuals for your pullman. Or make piles of shirts and pants for your backpack, and T-shirts and underwear for a small duffel. Also gather up things to pack in side pockets, like accessories and small items that might otherwise get lost in your bag.

Now you're ready to pack your bags. Different people have different techniques. Which one you prefer depends on the bag, the clothes, and your own personal taste. If you've got casual clothes to stuff in a duffel bag for a camping trip, take a tip from generations of military personnel and roll up your clothes, which can then be packed tightly. If you're taking nicer clothes in a rigid suitcase, you'll want to fold your items neatly along a crease. Some people pack in piles according to how they'll separate their clothing at their destinations—socks and underwear together (since they'll share a drawer in the hotel dresser), T-shirts and shorts together (sharing another drawer), button-down shirts and slacks together (since they'll all go in the closet). Other people prefer to pack chronologically, with the clothes they'll need soonest on top, and those they won't need until the end of the trip on bottom; this is a good technique to use if you'll be living out of your luggage rather than unpacking along the way.

However you choose to pack, start placing your clothes in your chosen bags. If everything fits in the bag you chose, you're good to go. If the bags are too big, reconsider your luggage selection. If the bag is too small, you'll need to decide whether to get a larger bag or remove some clothes.

Finally, carry each packed bag for several yards a couple of times. If a bag is too heavy, split the contents into two smaller bags; think of how you'll feel carrying it and repeatedly hoisting it in and out of your vehicle.

When you're done filling your bags, put your packing list inside your luggage. That way you'll have a ready-made checklist for the return trip, to make sure you don't leave anything behind.

Packing for Children

Making kids part of the packing process will help them feel like they're active participants in the trip, and it'll avoid horrible surprises on the road. ("You brought my white shorts?! I hate those shorts!") You can't let kids start their own packing lists from scratch, but you can let them choose specific items for a list you make. If your list includes seven T-shirts, let your child pick out which seven to bring. If your list includes one dressy outfit, let your child select one. Of course, you have veto power, but this gives your child a sense of some control. You can even pack side-by-side to make packing seem like a joint effort: "We'll need one nice outfit to visit Grandma. Daddy is bringing a white shirt and a necktie. What outfit do you want to bring?"

Children's luggage is another way to make your kids feel like they've got a part to play in your road trip. Teenagers can get their own bags and carry them themselves. But even smaller kids who can't carry their own suitcases might be able to carry a small bag with a

FOR THE BABY

Babies and young children may need all or some of the following:

- ☐ Car seat
- ☐ Carrier
- ☐ Bottles, bottle nipples, bottle brush
- ☐ Breast pump
- ☐ Teething rings and pacifiers
- ☐ Diapers
- ☐ Diaper-rash cream and baby powder
- ☐ Changing pad
- ☐ Cleansing wipes
- ☐ Blanket
- ☐ Bibs
- ☐ Your pediatrician's contact information

few of their personal items in it—perhaps a knapsack with toiletries, a toy, and one or two items of clothing.

Kids should also have a say in what games and other diversions will be brought along for the drive itself (see Chapter 4).

Consider including a few small, familiar items to help make your kids feel at home. Everyday things like a washcloth, bath toy, or night-light from home can go a long way toward relaxing your children in a new place.

My grandson Ethan's favorite bedsheets have a Thomas the Tank Engine cartoon on them. So whenever we go away, I pack his pillowcase in the suitcase and put it on the pillow wherever we stop—at motels or at his Aunt Jessica's house. It makes him feel more comfortable and helps him sleep in a place that's strange to him.

TRAVEL LOG

–Carol G., Albuquerque, New Mexico

PACKING CAR ESSENTIALS

Organizing the dozens of must-haves for your car is yet another kettle of fish. Categorize the necessities: navigator's materials; things you'll need for your comfort and entertainment while driving; a tool kit. Then divide these items into those that can be kept inside the car and those that should be stowed in the trunk.

The navigator's materials can be stacked neatly in the glove compartment, along with a pair of sunglasses for the driver in case the sun shifts. (If your glove compartment is stuffed with maps, clear out the ones you won't need.) The glove compartment is also a good place to store a tire pressure gauge and a couple of extra basic first-aid supplies, such as bandages and pain relievers. Pop in an ice scraper, too, if you'll be traveling somewhere cold; if it's left in the trunk you may have to dig under your luggage when the windshield needs clearing.

When it comes to the things that will enliven and ease your trip, think containment. Toys and activity supplies for your kids can be kept in clear plastic containers with tight-fitting lids. Tapes and CDs can be kept in plastic containers, media-specific carrying cases, or

FOR THE GLOVE COMPARTMENT

- ☐ Maps
- ☐ Flashlight
- ☐ Pen and paper
- ☐ Insurance and car registration
- ☐ Coins
- ☐ Basic first-aid kit
- ☐ Tire pressure gauge
- ☐ Ice scraper
- ☐ Rag
- ☐ Spare sunglasses

even a shoebox. CD organizers are particularly useful, since the sleeves replace the heavier, breakable plastic jewel boxes. Snacks or meals may fill a few resealable plastic bags or a cooler; be sure to bring an extra plastic bag for garbage, too. If you're traveling with pets, you'll need to stock your car with them in mind as well. (For details on food, suggested car activities, and pet needs see Chapter 4.) You may also want to add a couple of not-quite-packables to the pile: small pillows and a light blanket to help passengers, especially kids, sleep through the ride.

Pack emergency auto equipment in a box or tool bag so it doesn't get scattered. For a full list of emergency supplies, see Chapter 2.

LOADING YOUR VEHICLE

Some people like to pack their cars the night before they leave. If that helps you sleep easier, go ahead, but it shouldn't be necessary. Once you know how you're going to load your vehicle, it shouldn't take long at all to get ready in the morning.

Make a plan for loading your bags. What will go where? Will there be enough room? What bags will go on top and which on bottom?

Do a test loading if you're not sure it's all going to fit properly. If there's any reason to be concerned about the security of your car, stay on the safe side and bring your luggage back indoors after the test load. You don't want to wake up in the morning to find that all your bags are gone—especially after you spent so much time packing them!

In the Trunk

Take a minute to size up your luggage situation before you start loading your trunk. Make mental notes of any bags or items you might need to access on the road, anything fragile, and any other "special treatment" bags.

Start by loading the larger and less flexible luggage, including your emergency auto tool kit. Smaller and more squashable bags go in next, arranged around the larger pieces as necessary. Bags that you'd like to have in easy reach should be added toward the front of the trunk space. If you've got a garment bag or anything that would be damaged from the pressure of something else on top of it, place it on top.

Stash extra food and entertainment supplies in an easily accessible niche. If you're bringing coats, you may want to put them in the trunk as well. If you're traveling in very cold weather, however, you may want to keep your coats in the car with you. Then when you want or need to stop, you won't be stuck shivering as you try to retrieve your coat.

Inside the Car

Anything you'll need at arm's reach during the drive should be kept in the passenger area of your car. If you're not sure you'll need it, put it in the trunk; you can always get it out later. What you bring inside the car should be essentials you'll need on the road, not items for your destination. Remember, anything in the passenger compartment takes space away from passengers. The more you bring, the less room you've got.

Bring only as much food and as many toys as you'll need for the next few hours inside with you, and put the rest in the trunk.

On the Roof

The trunk isn't the only place to stow your luggage. You can put it on the roof, too. Many cars and SUVs come equipped with luggage racks. You can also request a luggage rack on a rental car.

The advantage is obvious: You miraculously create more space for your things. But you've got to be sure you're using it correctly, or your luggage won't be secure for long. Check your owner's manual for exact instructions, and test it out locally before you actually hit the road. If you're renting, ask the rental agent to show you how to use the rack properly. And always bring a few extra bungee cords of a length that will stretch across the top of the vehicle—available at any hardware store—in case you lose one along the way.

You can strap the luggage right onto the top of the vehicle or acquire a container to attach to the rack, into which you can load your luggage. The least expensive option is a canvas carrier. These carriers are collapsible and thus easy to store, but they're usually not fully waterproof. Hard-sided cargo containers are bulkier, but they're also watertight. Look for containers or carriers with internal straps to keep your items in place. Make sure the mounting hardware will work with your roof rack.

Specialty Racks

Chances are that your skis won't fit in your car, and neither will your family's bicycles. If you're going to be taking sporting equipment on a trip, look into buying or renting a rack. You can bring everything from your kayak to your snowboard along for the ride, which will save you plenty of money on renting equipment at your destination.

Some racks attach to your roof, while others attach to the rear of your vehicle. For all kinds of racks, look for

IN PRAISE OF CELL PHONES

They may be a nuisance when they're ringing during a movie, but on the road cell phones can be lifesavers. Here are some tips for making the most of a cell phone on the road:

▶ **Switch to a roaming plan:** If you've got local calling, a roaming plan might save you money for calls you make when you're outside your home area. You can switch back to your normal plan after you return.

▶ **Rent a phone:** If you don't own a cell phone, you can rent one short-term specifically for your trip.

▶ **Bring the hands-free attachment:** Talking on a cell phone without these attachments while driving is distracting and dangerous. In some places, it's also illegal.

▶ **Bring your recharger:** A cell phone is no good if it's dead. You'll need to recharge your phone every night on the road to make sure it's ready to go every day.

▶ **Check out cigarette lighter adaptors:** These can keep your phone juiced up while you're actually on the move.

▶ **Program your emergency numbers:** Why waste time fumbling for phone numbers? Program a few numbers before you leave: your auto club, your rental agency's 800 number, your health insurance hot line, the number of the motel where you're heading, or your Aunt Judy's house where you're spending the weekend.

models that will protect your equipment and absorb shock to keep vibration to a minimum. Roof mounts are generally the most versatile. For snow sports carriers, look for features like oversize buttons, which are easier to manage while wearing gloves. Trunk and hitch mounts both attach to the rear of your vehicle and can be easier to use, especially if you've got a tall vehicle. Hitch mounts for bikes are particularly easy to use; you'll need a receiver hitch on your car. And, of course, the market offers plenty of accessories to increase stability, add extra locks, reduce noise, and so on.

READY TO GO

For many people, packing is the most intimidating part of a trip. They're forever worrying that they'll forget something, throwing extra clothes in the suitcase "just in case," or trying to squeeze everything into a single overstuffed bag that Hercules couldn't lift. But with a little forethought, packing isn't an ordeal.

Proper packing requires a bit of planning ahead of time, but it'll help ease your mind once you've embarked on your journey. If you planned properly, you'll have everything you need—and nothing you don't need. So make your list, pack your bags, and you'll be ready to hit the road feeling prepared for what lies ahead.

4

PEDAL TO THE METAL

It's one of life's most important lessons: Getting there is half the fun. Your ultimate destination gives your trip a goal, an objective, an impetus. But the journey itself is equally significant. After all, you might spend as much time driving to and from your destination as you do actually being there.

If you view your time on the road as merely the price of getting from Point A to Point B you're bound to get frustrated or bored after a few hours. This is especially true on your way home, when instead of embarking on a new adventure you're heading back to your daily routines.

How can you make your trip more fun or interesting for you and your passengers? How do you avoid the pitfalls that can make driving an annoyance? Treat your travel time as part of the adventure, and you'll enjoy a richer, more rewarding experience.

PASSING THE HOURS

Even people who relish spending days on the road grow weary of racing the white stripe. No matter how beautiful the scenery, how fascinating your destination, and how dazzling your fellow passengers, at some point a road trip can seem like a really long drive—and little more.

There are two main ways to battle road fatigue: cut the time you spend behind the wheel and make the time you do spend there pass more quickly. If you juggle a bit of both, you'll be able to spur the hours along—an especially welcome acceleration if you've got kids in the backseat asking the eternal: "Are we there yet?"

Once you've charted your basic route, sketch out your driving schedule. When do you plan to leave in the morning? When do you hope to stop for the night? Where do you plan to stop along the way? Then put a little forethought into what might affect this schedule so that you're less likely to be caught in an exhausting situation.

Reducing Your Drive Time

When you drive is as important as where. Many inter-states are used not only by long-distance travelers but also by commuters. Since you don't want to waste time in rush-hour traffic on your vacation, check your route carefully. Try not to drive into or around a major city during morning or afternoon rush hours. You're better off getting up extra early to avoid a traffic jam at the beginning of the day. If you're coming up on a major city between 4 and 6 PM, you'll actually save time by stopping for an early dinner and waiting until the commute is over before heading into town.

Stay flexible if you run into traffic or construction. Instead of crawling along at 5 mph, take out your map and look for an easily accessible alternate route. Even if

---

Driving back down Cape Cod after our vacation, we got stuck in traffic because of an accident on the main road. I got very tense just sitting there until, after nearly an hour, I decided to pull off onto the slower side roads instead. We got to see a whole side of Cape Cod that we had always ignored—all the quaint towns off the highway. Traffic moved slowly, with lots of stops at traffic lights, but we still moved faster than we would have if we'd stayed on the main road, and we managed to relax and enjoy an unexpected side trip.

TRAVEL LOG

–Allan B., Bayonne, New Jersey

---

it's a roundabout way with slower speed limits, a side street that moves is quicker than an interstate that's jammed. If there's no alternative course, get off the road and stop to get a snack or to stretch your legs. A break can calm your frustrations and give the jam time to clear up. While you may add to your total travel time, at least you'll limit your stint at the steering wheel.

As Time Goes By

Your road map can tell you how many miles lie between you and your destination, but how long the trip will feel to you depends on variety and flexibility. Remember, you don't always have to stick with your plan. If the road starts to pall, vary your driving experience. Spend the morning meandering on back roads and pick up fresh corn and tomatoes at a farm stand, for instance, then pull onto the interstate to save time in the afternoon. Conversely, if you're running ahead of schedule on the highway, pull off and explore the smaller local roads for a while.

Factor frequent breaks into your daily plan. The basic rule of thumb: Stop every two hours to stretch your muscles, use a rest room, and have a snack. But varying the kind of break also helps time slip by. Rather than hitting a series of quick-serve rest stops, pull over spontaneously to linger over a fantastic view. You may be tempted to check out local handicrafts and produce, or to explore small towns along the way. All told, these stops may add an hour or two to your actual travel time each day, but they can make the drive feel shorter.

There's nothing better than the radio to help pass the time while you're on the road. On a spin through the stations you could strike a fount of local color. But what if on a morning drive you find the dial crowded with obnoxious shock jocks? What if you're stuck someplace where the only options are raving loonies with distasteful call-in shows? Or what if you can't get any stations at all?

Fortunately, tape decks and CD players are standard on many cars, and most rental car agencies offer them as options. So stock up on your favorite tunes before you head out on your trip. Just be sure to consult your fellow passengers to make sure you've chosen music that everyone in the car can live with.

Books on tape are another way to pass the time. You can find best-selling fiction, self-help books, or mystery novels on tape at your local library or bookstore. You could also try foreign language cassettes—you'll be surprised at how much vocabulary you can soak up over the course of a long car ride. Imagine driving to Québec City and being able to check in at your hotel in French, or driving to Tijuana, Mexico, and bargaining over blankets in newly learned Spanish.

Car games that require your imagination rather than a game board or a set of batteries are a good way to get everyone involved. If you keep track of who wins each round of a game, the ultimate winner could get a prize like choosing the next CD or deciding where you stop for dinner.

CAR GAMES

Besides the classics like I Spy and Twenty Questions, here are a few other games to try:

▶ **Rubberneckers:** This boxed deck of illustrated cards challenges you to spot specific things out of the car window—rack up points for each find to win.

▶ **Guessing mileage:** When passing a sign posting the number of miles until the next city or major destination, everyone predicts what the next mileage sign will say. The guessing range narrows as you approach the destination, and before you know it, you'll be there.

▶ **Adding adjectives:** Make up a basic sentence with a missing adjective, such as "He has a _____ face"; then choose a letter. Everyone takes turns coming up with an adjective that begins with the chosen letter; when people are baffled they drop out of the running.

▶ **The geography game:** One person names a place—a state, city, country, continent, river, or ocean—and the next person has to come up with another place that starts with the last letter of the first place. If Dad starts out with "Georgia," Uncle Al might follow with "Antwerp," and Aunt Betsy might come up with "Paris." As people get stumped, they're out of the game. Keep going until you have one winner.

▶ **50 states through license plates:** Everyone keeps his or her eyes peeled for cars with out-of-state license plates; the goal is to spot at least one license plate from every state.

The drive back home can often seem like more of a chore than the first leg of the journey. Keep this in mind when you've reached your destination, and pick up or reserve a few items for the return trip that will make it more interesting.

▶ **Buy some local music.** Pick up a country CD when you're in Nashville, or jazz in New Orleans, or hip-hop in New York City, and you'll bring a bit of your vacation home with you.

▶ **Pack a picnic of local goodies.** Put together a moveable feast of local specialties like cheese-steak sandwiches from Philadelphia, a bag of fresh oranges from Miami, or Ghirardelli chocolate and sourdough bread from San Francisco.

▶ **Collect souvenirs.** Special books or coloring books found in the places you've visited can keep your kids busy on the way home. Children can also create their own travel scrapbooks. During the trip, help them collect postcards, ticket stubs, and other mementos of the places they've seen; then, on the way back, they can organize and decorate them in a notebook.

▶ **Bring a page-turner.** On the first half of your drive, read part of a long and gripping book aloud, or listen to a section on tape. Save the end of the story for the return trip.

For anyone who's not in the driver's seat, nothing passes the time like sleep. If you've got at least three passengers, you can switch off who drives, who navigates (and helps keep the driver awake), and who gets to nap. If you've only got two people in the car, napping is still a possibility as long as the driver is alert and comfortable without a navigator for a while.

TAKING BREAKS

You'll need to take a break every couple of hours to stretch your legs; this is also a good time to switch drivers if you're taking turns. There are a couple of universal reasons to pull off the road, but you might need to take other breaks, or stop more frequently, depending on your route and your passengers. Whatever your reason for stopping, don't get out of the car only to sit in a restaurant booth. Take a walk and loosen up to prevent muscle cramps and circulation problems.

Getting Gas

Never let your gas fall below a quarter tank. When your gas gauge dips near a quarter tank, start looking for a place to fill up. You might want to scout out the lowest price or a branch of a particular chain, so you'll need a bit of leeway, especially if you run into any delays.

Although self-serve pumps are cheaper and usually faster than full service, sometimes it pays to stop for the latter. An attendant will check your oil and tires, and clean your windshield if asked. In some states, such as New Jersey, self-serve is unavailable.

Using the Rest Room

You can find the facilities at a gas station, restaurant, or rest area. If you've got kids in the car, anticipate Murphy's Law: the urgency to get them to a bathroom is inversely proportional to the likelihood of finding one. The plea "I gotta go!" usually arrives when you're in heavy traffic or have just left the only rest stop in a 50-mi radius. One solution is to insist that everyone in the car use the rest room whenever you stop for a break—whether or not nature calls. If young children balk, induce them with a treat if they'll "try." Also, watch your kids' liquid intake; try to time beverages for stretches when you're sure of having rest room options. Carry disposable wipes and a mini-roll of toilet paper, and you'll be able to brave a less-than-clean lav.

EATING ON THE ROAD

Your car can probably last half a day before it needs a fill-up. Your body can't wait that long. After several hours cooped up in a car, you'll need to refuel. Don't consign yourself to greasy spoons, though; you'll need meals that will nourish you over the next stage of your trip. Plan ahead, and you'll never find yourself running on empty.

If you'll be on the road for several days in a row, you'll need to make an overall eating plan. Will you grab fast food or head off the highway to find a restaurant? Will you save money by bringing your own meals or splurge a bit and explore local eateries? You've got options, and you can mix and match them: For instance, you might like to start your day with a hot breakfast at a diner but pack a nutritious cold lunch for the car. Whatever you decide, there are a few guidelines to keep in mind.

▶ Try to adhere to your usual meal schedule, as eating at irregular times can throw off your normal rhythms and make you tired, hungry, or grumpy.

▶ Try to maintain a healthy diet. Of course there will be exceptions, but make an effort to stay within the appropriate daily range of calories, fat, protein, and carbohydrates. If you veer out of your norm at one meal, get back on track at the next.

▶ Don't let yourself get too hungry. You'll leave yourself prone to headaches and light-headedness, and you're more likely to stuff yourself when you do stop to eat.

▶ Stop to eat. Even if you pack food for the car, it's better for your digestion to park somewhere and relax while you eat, as opposed to eating on the go with a sandwich in one hand and the steering wheel in the other.

Bringing Your Own Food

Eating at restaurants three times a day can be hazardous to your wallet—and your waistline. Packing your own food in a small cooler is the best way to save

PACKING A COOLER

☐ Water: Bring several small bottles that you've placed in the freezer overnight. Just be sure not to freeze *all* your water or you'll be waiting all morning for it to thaw.

☐ Other drinks: Most fruit juices and flavored waters are better alternatives than soda. Avoid drinks like cranberry juice and chocolate beverages that are especially sticky or can leave stubborn stains. Small bottles or punch boxes are easiest to transport and least likely to make a mess.

☐ Healthy snacks: Try apples, oranges, grapes, celery, baby carrots, raisins—anything that doesn't require any utensils to eat and doesn't stain (sorry, pomegranates).

☐ Guilty pleasures: Don't pretend you'll give up junk food entirely when you're on the road, but try to consume it in small amounts. Choose relatively healthy goodies, such as air-popped popcorn.

☐ Supplies: Paper plates, napkins, and plastic cups and utensils will come in handy if you pull over for a roadside picnic. Pack straws to help avoid spilling drinks in the car, and bring several plastic bags for garbage.

☐ Cooler packs: These small plastic packs are filled with a gel that stays cold much longer than ice, and they won't melt or spill.

money and to make sure you're eating right en route. Moreover, having food with you ensures that you'll have something to nibble exactly when you need it—a lifesaver if you've got kids in the backseat who are getting hungry. Finally, if you've got special dietary concerns, bringing your own food may well be the most practical option.

CROSSING BORDERS Carrying your own food can pose problems when you're crossing borders. Fresh, and sometimes packaged, food is closely regulated at international checkpoints, so consult the U.S. Department of Agriculture Web site to determine what you can carry when leaving and returning to the United States. Sometimes restrictions regulate transportation of fruits and vegetables across state borders, too; California, for instance, has numerous quarantines designed to eradicate fruit-borne insects. If you have any prohibited food items, you'll have to throw them away. Tell the truth about what you've got; bringing in forbidden items could prove seriously damaging to the place you're visiting and could land you a steep fine.

Eating Well at Restaurants

Eating healthy food is particularly important on a road trip. If you're driving or navigating, you'll need to keep your energy level up without falling prey to sugar highs and crashes. Since you'll likely be more sedentary than usual, you won't have the chance to burn off your normal amount of calories. And you don't want to trigger an attack of indigestion when you've got a long, unbroken stretch of highway ahead.

Don't relegate yourself to an unending stream of fried food, which would be both tiresome and unhealthy. These days you can order a relatively healthy meal even at most fast-food joints. National chains like McDonald's, Burger King, and Wendy's, for instance, have lower-fat and lower-calorie items such as pita sandwiches, salads, and grilled chicken, and they continue to increase the number of more healthful selections.

Neither are you at the mercy of a restaurant menu. Ask for a menu item to be grilled instead of fried, steamed instead of sautéed. Ask for salad dressing on the side, or a green salad instead of potato salad. Reconsider the meaning of "all you can eat" at a buffet restaurant. Also, control the condiments. Hold the cheese and bacon on your burger; put mustard on your sandwich instead of mayo. Such decisions are the easiest way to cut back on calories, fat, and sodium.

Road trips are the only time I ever eat fast food. I watch the signs for a Subway sandwich shop, because I know they have healthier food than the hamburger spots and diners. I can get exactly what I want on it, and they have a lot of decent options.

TRAVEL LOG

–Michael P., Parma Heights, Ohio

All this said, another tip for eating well on the road is to search out outstanding local specialties as you plan your route. Are you passing the cherry pie capital of the Midwest? Is the next town renowned for its barbecue? Perhaps a town or city on your route has a strong ethnic community whose cuisine intrigues you—now's the chance to try it. With such treats, you're not only varying your meals, you're literally tasting diverse local flavors. And isn't that one of the things a road trip is all about?

Saving Money

There's no way around it: Bringing your own food saves the most money. Even if you only bring beverages, you'll save several dollars a day. Maximize the amount of food you bring, and you'll spend the minimum at restaurants, snack bars, and rest stops.

When stocking a cooler with drinks and snacks for your trip, visit a bulk food warehouse to take advantage of their lower prices. If you're restocking en route, head to a supermarket, where prices are generally lower than at convenience stores or gas station minimarts. If you belong to a savings club at a particular supermarket chain, bring your club card with you; you'll be eligible for discounts at any branch of the chain. You may want to invest in a travel cooler and warmer; these plug into dashboard cigarette lighters and will keep liquids cool or warm as needed. (And remember not to leave sodas in your car in freezing weather.)

▶ **Use resealable beverage containers.** Bring along a few tight-fitting plastic lids to cover soda-can tops. Besides preventing spills, they'll help keep the carbonation fizzing. Otherwise, opt for bottles with twist-on caps, although these are more tip-prone.

▶ **Keep hot beverages like coffee in a container with a spill-proof lid**—either an insulated travel mug or a disposable coffee cup. Coffee not only leaves terrible stains but can also burn you.

▶ **Straws reduce spills.** Buy them in advance or take a few extras at a fast-food restaurant on your route.

▶ **Choose cups of normal size and put them in cup holders.** Supersize beverages might seem thrifty at first, but most people can't finish one before a cold drink gets warm. Also, supersize cups sometimes don't fit into standard cup holders; these half-filled behemoths are ripe for spillage when they're sitting on the floor or in a passenger's lap.

▶ **Double-cup paper cups.** Paper cups can soften and leak if liquid is left in them for an extended time.

▶ **Before you start driving, make sure all cups aren't overfilled.**

▶ **Give kids juice boxes instead of a thermos or cups.** A six-pack of juice boxes costs a bit more than a large bottle of juice with a stack of paper cups, but the spill-proof boxes are still cheaper than the cost of having your upholstery cleaned.

At times, you'll need to sacrifice convenience to save money. Pass up the restaurants along the interstates and instead look for an eatery in a town you're passing through. You're sure to find better bargains—or at least better food for the same price—if you're willing to venture even a mile off your route. Start looking before you get hungry, and watch the clock: Many restaurants offer discounts for early dinners or late lunches.

When you do dine out, opt for plain water with your meals. Other drinks can add a substantial amount to your bill.

Finally, take advantage of dining discounts for young children and senior citizens. Sometimes, a moderately priced family restaurant can actually be cheaper than a fast-food stand, once children's menus are factored in; toddlers may even eat free at these establishments.

TRAVELING WITH CHILDREN

When the Brady Bunch went on their road trip to the Grand Canyon, all the kids piled happily into the station wagon, eager to sing "Ninety-nine Bottles of Beer on the Wall" and "On Top of Old Smokey" until they reached their destination. In real life, family road trips are rarely this perfect.

This doesn't mean, however, that your road trip can't be a happy family vacation. Kids can be surprisingly adaptable to new situations, and they're probably more comfortable in a familiar car than they would be on a bus, airplane, or train filled with strangers. Chances are good that your kids will enjoy the trip, if you take their special needs into account.

As you decide on which car to drive, make sure children have enough room to be comfortable for a long ride. Just because your backseat can hold three kids on a 10-minute ride to soccer practice doesn't mean it's large enough to accommodate the same number of passengers for a long ride, with the addition of toys, food, and a couple of small pieces of luggage. If you think you'll be pinched for space, consider renting a larger vehicle. A sunshade to attach to a backseat window may be a good idea if your kids will be napping.

KEEPING YOUNGER KIDS BUSY

▶ **Coloring books.** Coloring is a great way to pass the time—you might even be able to find a coloring book about the places you're going to visit, or the place you just left. Crayons soften at 100°F, so be sure not to leave them in the car in hot weather or they'll leave a waxy film everywhere. Colored pencils are less mess-prone.

▶ **Stories.** If you have an extra adult who can read aloud, great. If not, be sure the books you pack are ones the kids can enjoy on their own, without disturbing the driver. Or you could pre-record yourself reading a favorite story, and play the tape in the car.

▶ **Dolls and stuffed animals.** These remind kids of home and help them sleep. A teddy bear can also give your kids someone to talk to or play with in the backseat.

Little ones need to stop at least as frequently as adults, if not more. If you're traveling with toddlers or preschool kids, your trip will probably take a third longer than it would without them, thanks to frequent and slower pit stops. If you've got a newborn who needs to be changed and fed frequently, figure your trip will take up to twice as long as normal. If time is of the essence, consider driving longer stretches when they're asleep, or after they've had a large meal—but stay flexible and don't push them past their limits.

When you do stop for a break, diffuse the crankiness with exercise. Bring a ball or Frisbee to get your kids running around, play tag, do jumping jacks with them, or shake their sillies out.

A few entertainment ideas work well for kids of almost any age. Individual tape or CD players with headsets allow each passenger to listen to his or her own music. Travel editions of board games are another good bet. It's easy to find checkers, chess, and backgammon sets with magnetic pieces that cling to the boards.

A video can also buy you at least an hour of relatively quiet time. Minivans and RVs often have television screens and VCRs built in; if your vehicle doesn't come with one, bring a portable TV/VCR with an adapter that plugs into the dashboard cigarette lighter. If you've got a laptop with a CD-ROM drive, you could pack that for watching DVDs. Either way, bring your kids' favorite videos plus a surprise selection or two, perhaps something involving the place you're going to visit.

▶ **Books.** Kids keep quiet when they're reading, and each child can choose his or her own favorite book. But be wary of carsickness, which is often exacerbated by reading. Books on tape are one solution, either for everyone to hear or to play on individual headsets.

▶ **Music.** If you enjoy the same music as your kids do, let your kids pick the tape or CD you listen to, or the radio station you choose. If you don't agree on music, bring portable stereos with headphones for your kids.

▶ **Handheld video games.** These games are a favorite for many kids, but be sure the sound effects can be muted; the bleeping and electronic jingles can get on everyone's nerves. Also be sure the games alternate with other activities; squinting at the small screen for several hours in a row isn't a good idea.

TRAVELING WITH YOUR PET

If your pet is part of your household, you wouldn't dream of taking a family vacation without him or her. Compared to planes, trains, or buses, cars are generally the most pet-friendly; you don't have to worry about fellow passengers' allergies or attitudes, you can stop as often as you like, and you don't have to treat your animal like a suitcase to be checked in the luggage compartment. Like a piece of luggage, though, your dog or cat should have an identification tag in case it gets away from you on the road; this means wearing a collar.

Your pet has special needs that human family members don't. Prepare your animal for the trip by taking short test-drives from home. Make sure your car has a clear, flat space for your animal or its carrying case, and bring a couple of your pet's favorite toys to make it feel more comfortable in this strange environment.

International borders have special restrictions on animal travel, so check to make sure you're allowed to take your pet on the road before you leave home. The U.S. Department of Agriculture has the information you'll need.

Ask your veterinarian about any necessary shots. Rabies vaccinations should be up to date (with a tag as verification), as some states require proof of vaccination before allowing pets entry. Other shots might be wise depending on where you're heading; Lyme disease is prevalent in the Northeast, and your animal should be vaccinated if you plan to spend time in that area outdoors. Your vet might also prescribe animal tranquilizers in case your pet gets anxious in the car, although the ASPCA does not recommend using sedatives on pets.

See Chapter 5 for further information on preventing pet illnesses on the road.

On the Road with Rover

A loose pet in the car can make a quick escape if someone opens a door and can become a dangerous projectile in an emergency. Special "seat belts" for dogs are widely available at pet stores. Cat carriers can often be secured with seat belts as well.

Take extra food and water for your animal, even for short trips; you can stop anywhere on the road if you're hungry, but most fast-food joints on the interstate don't carry Tender Vittles or Mighty Dog. If your pet eats canned food without a pop top, bring a can opener. Bottled water or water from home is best to drink, since many pets get diarrhea from strange water. Put only small amounts of food and water in bowls, since it might spill out when you take a sharp turn.

Cars don't maintain comfortable temperatures for long. Leaving your pet alone in a vehicle in hot or cold weather, even for short periods, is strongly discouraged. In warm weather, temperatures in cars quickly soar to extreme levels, causing your pet to suffer heatstroke or worse. In cold weather, temperatures in cars drop when the engine is shut off and your pet can become hypothermic or die. In moderate weather, it may be all right to leave your pet in the car for brief periods, but always leave at least two windows open slightly—not open enough for the animal to jump out—to provide a cross draft of fresh air. You might consider a solar-powered fan that fits snugly in the car window. Lock the doors and put on your emergency brake, since animals have been known to accidentally shift cars into gear.

DOGS Dogs are famous for enjoying car rides—sometimes they seem like they want to get behind the wheel themselves, or at least sit in your lap while you're driving. But it's safest for you and your dog to keep him or her in a crate or behind a mesh or metal pet barrier installed behind the front seat. Should your vehicle make any sudden movements, an unrestrained dog can endanger you and himself or herself. A crate is also helpful if your dog is anxious or jumpy on the road. A crate-trained pet might actually be soothed by its snug, familiar surroundings. You can help condition your dog to enjoy car travel by going on short drives together before your big trip. Instead of always heading to the veterinarian or the groomer, use the car to take your dog to a park or playground so he or she will learn to associate the car with fun outings.

Keep the temperature comfortable for your dog, checking for excessive panting or shivering. Air-conditioning may be refreshing to you, but it could feel like an icy draft to a dog. If warmth is a concern, you can bundle up your pooch in a dog sweater or even baby clothes.

Although many dogs love to put their heads through open windows, it's not a good idea. The American Veterinary Medical Association says it's a great way for your dog to get ear, eye, or nose injuries. Likewise, putting your dog in the flatbed of your pickup truck seems like a treat, but it can be extremely dangerous for your pet if you swerve suddenly, stop short, or get in an accident. Keep the animal restrained in the passenger compartment.

Water is essential for dogs, who tend to overheat and
dehydrate easily. Your dog's usual bowl will probably
spill during a bumpy drive. Instead, consider taking a
resealable plastic container. You can uncover it to offer
Fido a drink whenever you stop and periodically while
you're moving on a smooth road, then reseal it to prevent spillage.

Dogs also need to make frequent stops along the way
to stretch their legs and relieve themselves. Don't allow
your dog to run loose at a rest stop, though; he or she
could get lost or run into traffic. Use a leash and make
sure your dog stays close to you.

CATS Cats aren't usually enthusiastic about car rides.
A carrying case is a must; find a flat, stable place to put
it, not on the floor where road noises are amplified and
can terrify your favorite furball. Line the carrier with a
towel or newspapers, and bring spare lining in case of a
mess. Some carriers connect to seat belts, which helps
keep the crate from moving.

Some cats get a bit queasy from motion, so it's a good idea to feed them small amounts during the day and save most of their food for when you're out of the car. Most cats can last several hours without using a litter box, but it's best to be safe. Either place a small litter box in the back of the carrying case (where any spills will be localized and easy to clean), or bring a litter box along for your cat to use when you stop. If you don't have a sealable litter box, use a large plastic container filled with kitty litter.

Even if you've got an outdoor cat, you don't want him or her to run off at a roadside pit stop. Bring a harness and leash; while your cat might be miserable wearing it for a few minutes, it's better to live with an unhappy cat than to lose a content one.

OTHER ANIMALS Birds and small pets like gerbils, hamsters, and guinea pigs are accustomed to spending time in a cage, so they might be better at traveling than animals averse to confinement.

Travel can be stressful for birds; they're very susceptible to drafts and sudden changes in temperature and easily frightened by strange noises and surroundings. To keep your bird calm, cover the cage—your pet will think it's nighttime outside and will be more likely to sleep through the trip with minimal problems. Place the cage securely in a well-ventilated area away from drafts. Remove the water container from the cage to avoid spills and bring extra birdseed, as it may spill, too. At every rest stop, make sure your bird has an ample drink of water.

Hamsters, gerbils, and guinea pigs can travel in their usual cage or a small carrier. Give them something to gnaw on, and make sure the enclosure is escape- and chew-proof. Rather than putting spillable dishes of food and water in the carrier, feed your pets when you stop for a break. Resist the temptation to take your pets out of their cage while you're on the move; it's best to let them rest undisturbed to avoid causing them further stress.

TIME FLIES

When you first planned your road trip, you probably had high expectations about every part of the experience, including the drive itself. Whether the journey turns out to be a memorable adventure or so uneventful and effortless that it flies by, a bit of careful planning can ensure that the drive isn't a chore, a hassle, or a nightmare. And the driving byword of flexibility will do double duty should you—knock wood—have trouble on the road.

5

BUMPS IN THE ROAD

Maybe you'll be one of the lucky people who never encounter a single problem in your travels. Everything will go according to plan, and you'll reach your destination directly and on time.

But probably not. You can prepare thoroughly and make foolproof plans and still, through no fault of your own, hit a bump in the road. It may be a literal bump that gives you a flat tire or a figurative bump, like a carsick child. Or your plans could be sideswiped by an icy road or pea-soup fog. Almost everyone has something go awry on a trip. The key is to be ready when something happens.

Aside from major catastrophes, you can resolve many road problems yourself or with the help of an emergency roadside assistance service. Invest a little time in preparation, and in return you can anticipate a road trip with fewer worries.

GETTING LOST

You've planned out your route, and you've got your map handy. So how on earth did you end up on *this* road, going the wrong way?

Don't feel foolish if you get lost. Columbus got lost, too. Driving on unfamiliar roads can be confusing, especially if they're not well marked—something you'll encounter with surprising frequency. It doesn't help if you have a host of distractions: sun in your eyes, the glare of headlights, kids making noise in the backseat, road construction, or poor visibility.

But all that's important now is how to get back on track. There are several ways to reorient yourself and get moving again.

Figuring It Out Yourself

The first step in getting back to where you want to be is figuring out where you are now. Look for signs that tell you what road you're on, what town you're near, what intersection you're approaching. Without this information, you can't plot a way back to your planned route.

Next, find a place to pull over. Don't try to read a map while you're driving. Even if you've got a navigator, it's best to stop to study the map; by continuing you could go even farther out of your way. Try to pull over to a side street or well-lit parking lot. If you're traveling through a dark area and are hesitant to stop, find a main street and drive in one direction until you reach a well-lit place where you feel comfortable pulling over. If nothing else, pull over to the side of the road and put your flashers on.

Now you can take out your maps. First, locate where you are now and orient the map accordingly. (For instance, if you zipped past Smallville 10 mi back, hold the map so that Smallville is behind you.) Then find the place you need to be and plot the best way to get back on the right path. You may not need to backtrack; the next turnoff, for instance, could intersect with your desired road. Or you may have to turn around and go back to where you made the initial wrong turn.

Asking for Help

If you're lost, don't be embarrassed to ask for assistance. Getting lost is an innocent error. Staying lost, on the other hand, is a completely avoidable, major mistake. If you stubbornly insist on finding your own way, you could end up, three months later, in Buenos Aires instead of Atlanta.

Seriously, you can put yourself in a bad situation if pride prevents you from getting the skinny from locals. A wrong turn can take you into a questionable neighborhood, or you could narrowly miss a gas station just when you need to fill your tank.

Tollbooth operators, service station employees, police officers, and cab drivers are among the most reliable sources for accurate directions. Letter carriers, delivery people, and restaurant employees should also know the lay of the land.

When you do find someone to ask for help, be prepared to take a few notes. Don't simply ask how to get back to the point where you went astray. Instead, explain which road you were taking to your destination and ask how best to get back on track. It's possible that there's a quicker way to get to your ultimate destination than the one you had planned, such as a local highway rather than a crowded interstate. Ask about local landmarks; these can be helpful visual cues if you're following an unplanned and unfamiliar route. Jot down the given directions and tips. Above all, don't just nod through the explanation, drive away, and then ask a passenger, "Did you get that?"

MEN ARE FROM MARS . . . It's been fodder for legions of stand-up comedians, and the humor derives from a grain of truth: Men don't like to stop and ask for directions. The reason isn't exactly clear. Some people suggest that it's psychological, that men view it as a sign of weakness when they admit they're lost. Others suggest it's rooted in biology, citing brain studies that show men are naturally better spatial navigators and so need less help to find their way. Whatever the reasons, the gender split here appears to be real: According to a survey conducted for tire maker Bridgestone/Firestone, 64% of women ask for directions when they are lost, while only 29% of men do.

CAR TROUBLE

You probably won't see it coming. You had your car tuned up and checked before you left home, and you felt confident that your car was in good enough condition to make the journey—otherwise you wouldn't have hit the road, right? But no matter how careful you are, sometimes the road brings surprises. Car trouble is every driver's nightmare, since it can strike at the worst times in the worst locations.

If you feel utterly mystified when you check under the hood, take a few hours and learn how to solve a few of the most common problems yourself. Double-check your kit of emergency car supplies before you leave (see Chapter 2) and make sure that your spare tire is in good shape and sufficiently pressurized. If you don't already belong to an auto club, consider joining one for its on-call roadside assistance service.

Dead Battery

A dead battery can literally stop you in your tracks. Most often, you'll discover this problem after you've stopped to eat or spend the night somewhere; when you try to start your car you hear only a horrible silence instead of the engine's purr.

There may be a mechanical problem; the battery's alternator may have broken or its water level may be low. Human error, though, is the most likely cause. You may have left your headlights on when you stopped the car, or perhaps you didn't shut all the doors firmly and an interior light kept burning. Either way, you've got a dead battery on your hands.

The good news is that this setback can often be quickly and easily fixed. All you need is a set of jumper cables and someone willing to lend you a hand. With a set of cables and another vehicle that has a good battery, you can jump-start your car and be on your way.

If jump-starting doesn't work, you'll need to be towed to a mechanic. Your battery could be beyond a jump start, or there could be a problem with your starter, ignition, or output voltage regulator.

JUMP-STARTING YOUR CAR Getting a jump start is a simple process, but it's still a process. Be careful to follow every step, in precise order. You can jump-start any car from any other car, but avoid pairing a motorcycle and a car. The power sources aren't compatible and the jump start will damage the motorcycle's ignition system.

1. Open your hood and check to see if your battery is cracked. A cracked battery will explode if you jump-start it. If you see a crack, do not use your cables. (Cracks are generally, but not always, readily visible.)

Call your auto club or a tow truck and buy a new battery as soon as possible.

2. Check that your battery cables are tight and the posts are clean. If your cables are dirty and loose, that may be the root of the problem. Clean off any visible corrosion around the dead battery, since this inhibits the cables' ability to transfer electricity. Use a battery terminal cleaner, a kind of wire brush sold in auto-parts stores. If you're without, here's a hint worthy of Heloise: pour a little soda on the terminals and within a few seconds the carbonic acid will eat away any corrosion.

3. Remove any metal watches, rings, or necklaces you may be wearing; if they come in contact with the battery terminals you risk an electricity arc. Position the vehicles so the batteries are as close together as possible without the cars touching.

4. Put both cars in park and turn off their ignitions. Turn off everything in the cars—air conditioners, radios, radar detectors—and unplug cell phones and other appliances from the lighters. When the jolt of juice hits, all power should go into the battery.

5. Connect one end of the positive (red) cable to the positive post on the dead battery. Positive posts are always marked with a plus symbol.

6. Connect the other end of the positive (red) cable to the positive post on the good battery.

7. Connect one end of the negative (black) cable to the negative post on the good battery. Negative posts are always marked with a minus sign.

8. Connect the other end of the negative (black) cable to a solid metal part of the car with the dead battery; usually a clean nut on the engine block or part of the metal frame will do. Do not connect the cable to the negative post on the dead battery. Such a connection could cause a spark close to the battery, and since batteries release explosive gases, you'd risk an explosion.

9. Start the vehicle with the good engine, revving it up occasionally to send more power to the dead battery. After a minute or two, try to start the dead car. If it doesn't work the first time, you may need to wait another minute and try again.

10. When the dead car starts, you'll need to disconnect the jumper cables in the exact reverse order in which you placed them. If the engine dies again, don't try to jump-start it again. Call for assistance instead.

When I arrived in Boston and parked the car it was broad daylight, so I didn't even think to check the headlights. It turns out that I had switched them on when I went through a tunnel, and I **TRAVEL LOG** left them on unintentionally. When I came back to the car a few hours later, the battery was dead and I had to push the car down the street into a gas station.

–Scott H., Great Neck, New York

Flat Tire

Sometimes it's a loud bang, and other times it's a slow hiss, but either way a tire deflating is one of the sounds you dread hearing. Don't despair. Provided you're prepared, you can change the tire yourself.

You'll know you have a slow leak if one side of your car starts dipping slightly and the steering gets spongy. It's easier to retain control over your car with an air leak than with a blowout; turn on your hazard lights, brake slowly, and ease off the road. A blowout may be preceded by a thumping sound. If your tire suddenly goes, ease your foot off the gas and grasp the steering wheel firmly until the car is under some control. Brake slowly and carefully and pull off the road. In either case, do not slam on the brakes; this may make you lose control of the car.

A little elbow grease can set you straight as long as you're comfortable doing a bit of roadside work. If you don't feel safe where you are, put on your flashers once you're on the shoulder and drive very slowly along the shoulder until you can reach help at a service, police, or fire station. Your tire may get chewed up beyond repair, but better safe than sorry.

If you've got a slow leak, you might want to try sealing the leak with a tire fixative, available in a small can at any auto-parts store. These cans have a short hose attached to the top; screw the nozzle onto your tire's air valve and squeeze the cap. Pressurized air and a sealant will fill your tire enough for the drive to a service station. If your tire is severely damaged, though, you will need to change it.

You may have a full-size spare tire or a compact mini-tire (commonly referred to as a "doughnut") that often comes with a car. Mini-tires are not meant to be driven for a long period. You should use it merely to drive straight to a gas station or auto shop to buy a new, full-size tire (and dispose of your flat). In fact, even if you've got a full-size spare tire, buy a new spare as soon as possible; just because you've just gotten one flat doesn't mean you won't get another one. Lightning does strike twice.

CHANGING A TIRE As you pull off to the side of the road, look for a straight section of highway and flat pavement where your car won't roll. Put your car in park (or in gear if you're driving a manual transmission) and set your emergency brake. If you're on a slope, put a chock, such as a tire block or a large rock, behind the wheel diagonally across from the flat tire. Grab your tools—lug wrench, jack, and a flashlight if necessary—and your spare tire, and follow these directions in order.

1. Block the tire opposite your flat (i.e. behind the left front tire if your right front tire is flat), using a tire block or a rock. This will keep your car from rolling when you raise it.

2. If you've got a hubcap, remove it. You can easily pry it off with the flat side of your lug wrench.

3. Starting at the top, loosen the lug nuts by gripping them with the wrench and turning the wrench counterclockwise. (Remember the mnemonic: righty tighty, lefty loosey.) Skip every other nut, loosening the first, third, and fifth on the first pass and the second and fourth on the next pass. This makes it easier for you to keep track of how many you've loosened and it uniformly secures the tire to the wheel. If the nuts are on very tightly, you may need to step down on the lug wrench with your foot. Do not remove the nuts yet.

4. Position your jack under the car's jacking point. Most cars have a jacking point—a notch or plate—just behind the front wheels and in front of the rear wheels. This is designed to hold the car's weight evenly when you jack it up. If you can't find the jacking point, consult your car's owner's manual. Make sure the jack rests on a firm, level surface; if the ground is soft or muddy, place a piece of wood underneath the jack.

5. Raise the car until your tire is a few inches up, just clearing the ground.

6. Remove the lug nuts completely and take them off the bolts.

7. Jack the car up a few more inches; then grab the wheel and pull the tire toward you, off the car.

8. Position your spare tire in front of the wheel well, and align the holes in the center with the bolts on the car. Then lift the tire into position on the bolts and push it onto the car as far as it will go.

9. Replace the lug nuts and tighten them with your fingers in the same order you loosened them, until all the nuts are firmly in place.

10. Lower the car using the jack until the car rests on all four tires. Tighten the lug nuts further with the lug wrench; then remove the jack.

11. Give the lug nuts a final tightening with the wrench so that they're completely secure.

12. Replace the hubcap by putting it back in place and tapping it with the heel of your hand.

13. Remove the tire block and put all your tools back in your car, along with the flat tire.

Overheated Engine

It's most likely to happen in summer, when your air-conditioning's on, or climbing steep hills. The first sign might be a temperature light or gauge on your dashboard, or it might be steam rising from your hood. Either way, you've got an engine that's overheating, and that's something that needs to be dealt with immediately.

First, turn off your air-conditioning and turn on your heater—yes, it may feel uncomfortable, but it could help save your engine. Then, find a safe place to pull off the road, put on your hazard lights, and turn off your engine. Lift your hood—using a rag or towel, since it may be hot to the touch—and take a look. There are many different causes for overheating, and these need to be treated accordingly. If you see a major leak of rusty water or radiator fluid, a ruptured hose, cracked radiator or radiator cap, or broken fan belt, do not try to continue driving. You'll need to call for help.

If nothing appears to be broken or leaking, you are most likely simply low on coolant fluid. This is simple enough to remedy by adding water to the radiator, but you will need to wait about 30 minutes for the engine to cool down. Never remove a radiator cap when the engine is hot or warm, as you may damage your vehicle and injure yourself when pressurized coolant boils over. Never pour cold water on the radiator in an effort to cool it down faster—you can seriously damage the car. You'll just have to be patient and wait for things to cool down naturally.

Once the radiator is cool, use a rag or towel to *slowly* remove the radiator cap. Add water to the overflow reservoir, the quart-size plastic bottle near the radiator. Then replace the cap, close the hood, and drive—without air-conditioning—to a gas station to check your fluids and make sure everything is in working order again.

Other Car Troubles

Other car troubles are common enough, but they're not ones you'll be able to fully solve yourself. You'll need to get yourself off the road and alert other drivers to the problem.

If you have no choice but to pull over, put on your hazard lights. Find a good place to pull over; a gas station is ideal, but a roadside diner is better than the shoulder. You can easily place a call to your auto club or a service station; you'll also be happier and safer having a meal or a milk shake while you wait for the tow truck than you would be sitting at the side of the road.

It's easiest to call for help from a cell phone. Otherwise, you'll need to walk to a pay phone or highway call box. Be extremely careful of traffic while walking along the shoulder, especially on large roads, where drivers may not expect to see pedestrians. Make note of road signs, landmarks, exit numbers, or nearby towns so that you can tell a tow truck or police officer where your car is.

If you're stuck roadside at night, light a safety flare 300 ft behind your car and a second one 10 ft behind—but do not light flares if you see spilled flammable fluids (oil, gasoline) on the ground or smell fumes coming from your vehicle. If you tie a white cloth to your car antenna, this will alert passersby that you're in distress. You should wait for someone to stop and help—a police officer or a good Samaritan. If you absolutely need to leave your car, take a flashlight and walk along the shoulder, being careful of passing traffic. Before you leave the car, extinguish safety flares by tapping them on the ground; never step on a lit flare.

Following is a rundown of how to handle various other car-related mishaps:

▶ Brake failure: Pump the brake pedal to build pressure. If that doesn't work, slowly apply your emergency or parking brake and shift your car into a lower gear.

▶ Stuck gas pedal: Try to pull the pedal back up with your toe. (Don't reach under the dashboard to loosen it by hand or you'll lose sight of the road.) If it's still stuck, shift into neutral or put in the clutch and brake gently.

▶ Blocked vision: If the hood latch fails and the hood flies up to block your view, roll down the window, turn on your emergency flashers, and pull off the road, looking out the window for guidance. If you're in the inside lane of a major highway and don't think you can get across several lanes of traffic, stay in your lane and brake gradually to a stop.

▶ Steering failure: Turn on your emergency flashers, ease your foot off the gas, and brake slowly to a stop.

▶ Headlight failure: Switch on the trusty emergency flashers as well as your parking lights and/or turn signals as you pull over to the side.

HAZARDOUS DRIVING CONDITIONS

Inclement weather and extreme temperatures call for modifications in the way you drive. In some conditions you may have to stop driving entirely. If you're driving in an unfamiliar area, you may run into conditions you're not used to driving in. Everyone's heard jokes or complaints about drivers from California becoming unglued in the face of a snow flurry, but imagine yourself in a similar situation. Be particularly cautious of both your own driving and others on the road; slowing down is better than losing time over a fender bender—or worse.

DRIVING IN RAIN The first rule of thumb: If you need to use your wipers, put your headlights on as well. When rain begins to fall, oil and other substances on the tarmac loosen and create a slippery layer, particularly within the first half hour or so of rain. This layer can compromise your tire traction. You may need to drive under the speed limit; take curves significantly more slowly than usual. If you hydroplane—skid on the road's slick layer of moisture—take your foot off the gas and steer in the direction of the skid to ride it out. If your rear wheels go right, for instance, turn your front wheels to the right, and vice versa. When you gain traction again, straighten the wheels. Never hit your brakes when skidding.

DRIVING IN FOG Some of the worst road accidents happen when motorists drive into a bank of thick fog and add to a pileup of cars hidden in the vapor. Don't drive into such a blind dead end. If you encounter thick fog, hit your turn signal, pull over cautiously, and wait for the fog to pass. If the fog isn't too heavy and you can still see your surroundings, switch on your fog lights and low beams. (The light from high beams will just reflect off the mist.) Watch carefully for headlights or taillights of other drivers.

COLD-WEATHER DRIVING Ice, snow, and extreme cold add several extra considerations to a road trip. As you prepare for your drive, equip your car with winter windshield wipers (with rubber coverings to keep ice from collecting on the blades) and nonfreezing windshield wiper fluid. Get a good-quality wiper fluid; the inexpensive blue stuff that claims to stay liquid until -30°F can actually freeze around 0° F. Keep in mind that car batteries lose power as the temperature drops; is your battery able to start a cold car with thick oil? Consult with a mechanic, and also have the mechanic check the engine's coolant levels. Tire chains will increase traction if you'll be facing snowy or icy roads, or you may want to invest in snow tires.

When packing supplies for your car, add a blanket and extra warm clothes to your list, in case you get stranded. Also bring a bag of sand; you can scatter it on snow or ice for better traction. Have a pair of sunglasses on hand; snow glare can tire your eyes.

If you've got a car with rear-wheel drive, you can increase traction by loading heavy items in the trunk. If you've got a front-wheel-drive car, try not to overburden your trunk with heavy items.

When you're ready to go, make sure that the windshield and all windows are deiced and clear. Start driving slowly and test your brakes with measured strokes to determine how much traction you have. Drive more slowly than usual, and brake early at intersections. Be wary of patches of that hard-to-spot "black ice." Bridges, overpasses, and shaded spots may stay icy after the rest of the roadway is dry and clear. Try to have at least a half tank of gas at all times.

If you do get stranded, make sure that your exhaust pipe is clear and then stay in your running vehicle. Crack your window to get some fresh air; you don't want to risk carbon monoxide poisoning.

HOT-WEATHER DRIVING If you'll be traveling in extreme heat, be sure to double-check your cooling system ahead of time. Bring a reflector shield that you can prop in your windshield when you stop. Also check your spare tire; extreme heat is hard on tires, so a spare in good condition is crucial. Bring plenty of extra water—at least one gallon per person per day—and a spray bottle. If you run low on water, you can conserve it while staving off thirst by spraying it into your mouth, rather than taking a full drink. Avoid alcohol and caffeine, since they dehydrate. Watch for signs of heat exhaustion: heavy sweating, clammy skin, and weakness or dizziness. Should you get stranded, stay with your car. You can use the horn and lights to signal for help, and more importantly, you'll need the vehicle's shade and shelter.

HIGH WINDS High winds don't usually cause a problem if you're driving a car, but if you're towing a trailer or steering an RV, strong winds can buffet you on an open road. Slow down; if you're in an exposed area and gusts start knocking you around, decelerate and correct your position as necessary.

ACCIDENTS

Accidents happen to even the safest of drivers; anyone can make a mistake on the road. Recent U.S. statistics from the Federal Highway Administration found well over 6 million traffic accidents in a single year. The good news is that more than two-thirds of these accidents involved property damage alone, and fatalities resulted in only one-half of 1%. If you know how best to react if an accident happens to you, it doesn't necessarily have to spell the end of your trip.

Drifting

It has happened to nearly every driver: you drift to the right and the wheels slip onto the shoulder. Keep this slipup from turning into a full-blown accident by coming to a stop rather than trying to get right back on the tarmac. If you overcorrect your steering, your car may snap left more quickly than you'd anticipated when the wheels reach the pavement—potentially sending you into another vehicle. Instead, grip the steering wheel firmly, take your foot off the gas, and brake slowly. Check your mirrors to see when you can safely pull back onto the road.

Fender Benders

Every accident is cause for alarm, but if the vehicles involved are still in driving condition and the people involved are not injured, a collision can end up being a relatively minor inconvenience.

No matter how minor the accident, never drive away until you have conferred with the other driver. This can turn a small incident into a felony if someone was hurt. Pull off the road as soon as you can, turn off your car, and put on your blinkers. If it's nighttime, you should light safety flares behind your car—one 300 ft behind and a second 10 ft behind.

Check for damage on all vehicles involved, and take notes on a piece of paper. Call the police using a cell phone or call box by the roadside, even if the accident seems trivial. The police will file a detailed accident report; this ounce of prevention safeguards you from being blamed for unrelated dents and dings by the other party. The police will also make note of any apparent physical problems and call for medical assistance if necessary.

While you're waiting for the police to arrive, you'll need to obtain certain information. Ask to see the other driver's license and write down the person's name, address, and driver's license number. Get his or her phone number and license plate number, and exchange insurance information, including insurer, policy number, and the insurance company's phone number. Write down where and when the accident occurred and the make, model, year, and color of all cars involved. If there were any witnesses, take down their names and phone numbers, too.

After the police have made a report, make sure your car is in working condition; if not, the police can call a tow truck for you. Extinguish any lit safety flares by tapping them on the ground. Contact your insurance company as soon as possible if you plan to file a claim.

TAKING PICTURES A camera could be a big help if you get into an accident. Snap shots of your car, with close-ups of the damage and full photos of the whole vehicle to show which areas are *not* visibly damaged. It could be useful in case there's any dispute over insurance claims, repair bills, or medical expenses. Take photos of all parts of the other party's vehicle as well, if someone else was involved in the accident. Also take pictures of any visible injuries.

I was driving with friends through Pennsylvania when a deer jumped directly into our SUV, crushing the bumper. We didn't have a regular camera but I did have a digital video camera, which I used to document the dead deer and its effect on our car. Not the most pleasant footage, but at least we had something to show the insurance company.

TRAVEL LOG

–Anneliese P., New York, New York

Major Accidents

If an accident leaves your car in undriveable condition or leaves any passengers injured, you'll still need to follow the same basic process as you would in a fender bender. There are, however, a few additional things to consider.

All injuries may not be immediately evident. Do not try to move a severely injured person by yourself, since you may inadvertently make the injuries worse. Instead, call an ambulance and wait for trained personnel to deal with medical emergencies. People with minor injuries should still be checked by paramedics and taken to a hospital if necessary; something that seems like a headache now might turn out to be a concussion, and what feels like a sprained muscle could be a broken bone.

In addition to the usual information you'd exchange in case of a minor incident, also take down the name and phone number of the hospital any injured people are taken to, and the name and phone number of the facility where any undriveable vehicles are being towed.

You will probably need to readjust your travel plans. Call ahead and alter or cancel any reservations, and inform anyone you were planning to meet about what has happened. You will most likely need to find accommodations nearby; when you know where you will be spending the night, give police contact information where you can be reached. If your car can be repaired quickly, you'll need to call your insurance company to find out what's covered and locate a nearby mechanic. If your car is totaled, your insurance company may provide a loaner vehicle until your claim is processed. If you've had an accident in a rental car, call the agency and find out what's covered and, if applicable, how and where you can get a replacement vehicle to finish your journey.

OTHER DANGERS If an accident results in power lines falling on your vehicle, stay inside the vehicle until help arrives and do not touch anything metal so that you do not get a severe electric shock. However, if fire is an immediate danger, you will have to jump clear without allowing any part of your body to touch the vehicle and the ground at the same time.

If your car plunges into a body of water but doesn't sink immediately, open a window to get out. An emergency escape hammer with a recessed blade, available at auto-parts stores, can crack the windows and cut through seat belts if such steps are necessary. If your vehicle begins to sink quickly, you will not be able to open a door to get out until the water pressure on the inside of the car matches the water pressure outside. The weight of the engine will usually sink the front of a car first, so move to the back, where you'll most likely have an air pocket. Exit from a rear window or door.

HEALTH PROBLEMS

You can't prepare for everything that could possibly go wrong, but you can prepare for the most common health issues travelers face. If you think taking precautions is unnecessary—"they have drugstores in Illinois, too, so why bother?"—remember that once you come down with a headache or motion sickness, a 20-minute search for the nearest pharmacy can seem like an eternity.

PACKING A FIRST-AID KIT

A small first-aid kit can fit in your purse, knapsack, glove compartment, or toiletries kit. With just a few key items, you can be prepared for the most common health problems you might encounter on the road. Here are the foundations of a first-aid kit:

- ☐ Antacids, laxatives, and diarrhea medicines
- ☐ Antibiotic ointments
- ☐ Bandages
- ☐ Cold medicine
- ☐ Cortisone cream
- ☐ Moleskin for blisters
- ☐ Motion sickness medication
- ☐ Nasal spray
- ☐ Prescription medications, if any
- ☐ Pain relievers, such as aspirin, acetaminophen, or ibuprofen
- ☐ Scissors
- ☐ Tissues
- ☐ Tweezers

Be sure to pack a first-aid kit for the car. Pack it with items you might need if you catch a cold or get minor burns or cuts, and also include treatments for maladies travelers often encounter, such as indigestion, blisters, or headaches. If you've got prescription medications for any frequently recurring illness, be sure to pack these, too.

Do not drive while taking any medication that will make you drowsy. Check warnings on both prescription and over-the-counter medications.

Motion Sickness

Everyone knows you can get seasick on a boat, but it's also common to get motion sickness in a car. Motion sickness is caused by the confusion in the brain between visual cues (what you're seeing) and the information detected in the inner ear (what your body is feeling). If your kids are sitting in the backseat playing a video game, they aren't noticing that they're moving at 50 mph, but their inner ear senses the movement and sends messages to the brain. The central nervous system reacts to this confusion by signaling the nausea center in the brain.

Anything from a bumpy road to an overheated car can bring on motion sickness. Kids are particularly susceptible. One of the major causes of nausea in cars is reading; this can be somewhat alleviated by keeping the reading material at eye level rather than in your lap. If you know you have difficulty reading in cars, stick to other things for entertainment such as music, car games, or books on tape, and try to plan out routes during your off-road breaks.

If you're susceptible to car sickness, you can prevent it in a few ways. Over-the-counter medications like Dramamine and Bonine help suppress the queasiness, but they may also make you drowsy; they're better for passengers than for drivers. The drug scopolamine is

CAR SICKNESS

In addition to over-the-counter medications, there are a few tried-and-true tricks that can help passengers overcome car sickness:

▶ **Sit in front, where you will feel less motion.** Keep your body and head as still as possible.

▶ **Fix your eyes on a distant object.**

▶ **Get plenty of fresh air as soon as you feel ill.** Open windows or at least set the air conditioner to draw in air from the outdoors.

▶ **Don't drink alcohol or smoke before getting in a car,** as both can exacerbate the symptoms of motion sickness.

▶ **Keep some crackers handy to munch.** An empty stomach makes motion sickness worse.

available in a pill or a patch and doesn't make you as drowsy, but it requires a prescription. Whatever medication you choose, you'll need to take it an hour before you get in the car.

Driver Fatigue

Sitting behind the wheel for hours on end can trigger headaches, backaches, and fatigue. You can reduce the likelihood of these problems with a bit of planning.

Headaches are easily treated with pain relievers, but you can help prevent them by wearing sunglasses dur-

STAY HEALTHY

Here are some tips for staying healthy on the road:

▶ **Avoid long drives during your normal sleeping hours.** Your alertness naturally diminishes during this time, and the disruption of your usual pattern could undermine your health.

▶ **Exercise along the way with a short jog or brisk walk during a break.** You can also do isometric exercises behind the wheel. For instance, arch your lower back while grasping the steering wheel; stretch your neck while keeping your eyes on the road; point an elbow toward the ceiling to stretch your tricep; and fan out your fingers.

▶ **Take a hint from the U.S. Department of Transportation.** The law prohibits truck drivers from being on the road for more than 10 hours a day. Don't extend your driving time longer than this.

ing daylight hours, flipping up your rearview mirror to avoid staring directly into headlights after dark, and getting fresh air by rolling down your windows. Don't let yourself get hungry for the sake of making good time, either, since this can also lead to headaches.

Protect your back by adjusting your seat, steering wheel, and mirrors so you're comfortable. Bring a small pillow for added lumbar support in your lower back. And never sit on your wallet when you're driving—take it out and put it in the glove compartment.

Sitting on a bulky wallet puts your spine out of alignment and strains your back after a short time.

Fatigue has many causes, including inadequate sleep, dehydration, and boredom. To combat fatigue, rest up before you go and relieve the monotony of long drives with music, breaks, and other diversions (see Chapter 4). And drink plenty of water—it's better for you than caffeinated beverages, which can actually dehydrate you further, or sugary drinks, which can give you a "sugar crash." If you find you need lots of caffeine to stay alert, you're too tired to continue. Don't risk dozing off behind the wheel; instead, find a place to rest as soon as possible, for the night or just for a few hours.

Getting Medical Attention

If you've got a medical problem that you can't treat with your first-aid kit, you'll need to find medical assistance.

Locals are the best source of information on where you can find medical help. Pull into a rest stop, gas station, or police station and ask where to find help. Hospitals are indicated on nearby major roads with blue-and-white signs marked "H." You can also call your health insurance provider, which could have a list of approved physicians in other cities, or may at least help you locate a doctor on the road. The insurance company might recommend a specific doctor or clinic, or advise you to visit an emergency room for a more serious problem.

Check with your health insurance provider before you leave home if you're planning to cross international borders, because not every policy will cover you outside the United States. If yours doesn't you can find short-term travel insurance that will fill this gap in your coverage.

Caring for Your Pet

The most common problems pets experience on car trips relate to temperature: hypothermia in cold weather and heatstroke and dehydration in hot weather. Don't leave your pet alone in a vehicle in either hot or cold weather; temperatures inside the vehicle can change quickly, and pets are very susceptible to such fluctuations. Hypothermia is manifested by prolonged shivering; prevent it by keeping your pet warm in the car, perhaps with an extra covering. You can avoid dehydration—indicated by dry mouth and sunken eyes—by bringing plenty of water and a water bowl in the car and monitoring your pet's liquid intake. Heatstroke will cause a dog to pant uncontrollably and froth at the mouth; it can be prevented by keeping your car cool and giving your pet plenty of cool water to drink. If your pet displays signs of any temperature-related illness, take it to a vet immediately.

Animals are also susceptible to motion sickness, evidenced by excessive drooling and vomiting. A carrying crate alleviates this problem for some animals; drugs are available from veterinarians for others. Many people have also had success with Rescue Remedy, which is a mix of flower essences.

See Chapter 4 for more detailed information on traveling with pets.

SMOOTH SAILING

If you're one of the lucky few, you won't hit any bumps in the road. You'll reach your destination directly, with your car purring like a kitten and all your passengers feeling fine.

But knowing that a snag is far from impossible, factor in this likelihood as you make your plans. Add some extra time to your itinerary so that it doesn't fall apart if you're running an hour late because you had to change a flat tire or took a wrong turn. If you're prepared for a few hitches, you won't have to throw in the towel—instead you'll put them behind you.

6

HITTING THE HAY

It might be a romantic guest house nestled in the woods or a budget motel alongside an interstate. Perhaps you'll pamper yourself with a luxury hotel or rough it on an air mattress in a friend's basement. Whether it's a home away from home or just a place to catch 40 winks, you'll need somewhere to spend the night at the end of a long day's drive.

If you're like most other travelers, you'll want to arrange your accommodations beforeleaving home. Whether you reserve a room at a favorite hotel, confirm a spot at a campground, or remind Aunt Zelda to leave the light on, remember to get specific directions and to give your estimated arrival time.

Before you make that reservation, decide on your lodging priorities. If you're on a budget, you'll probably seek inexpensive accommodations. If you're pressed for time, location may be preeminent and you'll want a place near the highway rather than in the center of town. And if you're traveling with kids, a pool or game room may top your wish list.

Even if you decide to hit the road without making advance reservations, you'll still need to plan a bit. Bring along books and newspaper, magazine, or Internet articles so that you'll have some resources at hand when you start searching for somewhere to bed down for the night.

PLANNING AHEAD VS. BEING SPONTANEOUS

Which do you value more, the security of knowing where you'll be spending the night or the thrill of finding a place on the spur of the moment? Spontaneity has its advantages: It's more adventurous and it can allow you more flexibility. On the other hand, when it's midnight and you're still driving from one motel to the next in search of a VACANCY sign, the exhilaration may evaporate.

Planning Ahead

If you need to be in a specific place—Galveston, not Corpus Christi—then make reservations in advance so you'll be sure of a bed there. Ditto if you've got a limited budget. It won't matter if you find a dozen high-end hotels with empty rooms if you've only got enough cash for a Motel 6. It's also best to have a definite booking if you'll be driving a long day and don't want to waste time and energy hunting for a room.

Planning ahead is preferable too if you're traveling with kids. You can reduce fidgeting with the lure of a treat at the end of the day, such as a favorite cable TV show or a swim in an indoor pool. Plus, you'll be able to give them a definite answer when they start asking, "Are we there yet?"

Being Spontaneous

Looking for a place on the road is easier than you think, especially if you're not constrained by a tight budget or a particular location. Aim to begin your search before sunset so that you can get a good look at your potential lodgings—and possibly beat other spontaneous types to the punch. Ask people along the way—at gas stations, restaurants, and rest areas—if they have suggestions in your destination; you might find a lovely bed-and-breakfast a few miles off the road that you'd never have stumbled across on your own.

Roadside motels often advertise vacancies on their signs, so you won't have to pull off the road to inquire within. If you're looking for something quieter, more unusual, or with some local character, venture into the nearest town. Exits from interstates and other multi-lane highways typically have signs pointing to nearby accommodations.

Don't hold out for the perfect place—just look for a place that's fine for the night. And set a time limit to your search, such as: "If we don't find a cute B&B by 8 PM, we'll settle for the next cheap motel we find."

The Best of Both Worlds

There is a way to keep a bit of freedom without playing it completely by ear: Make same-day reservations. Bring a guidebook with thorough coverage of the lodging options in the area you're visiting. Each morning before you leave, figure out where you'd like to stop that evening, and book a room in that town for the evening. That way, you can create your travel plans en route and still have peace of mind.

This scenario is especially simple if you're staying at a chain motel or hotel that you like. The desk clerk at a Holiday Inn in Kansas City can call ahead to make a reservation for you at the Holiday Inn in St. Louis and give you exact directions on how to find it.

Saving Money

Consider the following points shrewdly and you'll be able to keep your lodging costs down.

▶ **Location:** Save money by staying outside major cities and off major highways.

▶ **Timing:** Motels near vacation areas might offer off-season discounts. Luxury hotels in major cities often cost a fortune for midweek business travelers, but they're a steal on the weekends.

▶ **Discounts:** You may be eligible for savings because of your age, corporate affiliations, or club memberships. Many chains offer discounts in conjunction with credit-card companies, rental car agencies, or frequent-flyer programs. There are often bonuses for multinight stays, such as a fourth night free when booking three. Calling in advance or checking on-line can also yield substantial savings over the official "rack" rates. Make sure to ask the reservation agent for the lowest possible rate, which can sometimes be lower than a corporate or AAA discount rate.

▶ **Extras:** If breakfast is included, it could save you the cost of a restaurant meal. A pay-per-view movie might cost $10, but it's cheaper than taking several people to a movie theater.

▶ **Bring your own:** Take your kids' handheld electronic game and forgo the pay-per-play video games in your hotel. Use your cell phone rather than the room phone. Hotels generally charge $1 and up for a local call and tack on a surcharge of as much as 55% for long-distance calls. Bring your own sodas and snacks instead of eating the overpriced items in your hotel minibar or vending machine.

▶ Sharing: When inquiring at guest houses, inns, or B&Bs, ask about rooms with shared bath. These generally have a lower rate than rooms with private bathrooms.

Traveling with Pets

Whatever type of accommodations you choose, check in advance to make sure pets are allowed and welcome. For the sake of your hosts, always ask where to walk your animal outside. Never leave your pet alone in your room unless you're certain it will not disturb other guests. If you're staying in a hotel, pick a room on the ground floor, which is more convenient for late-night walks. For reviews of hotels countrywide that welcome pets, check out *Fodor's Where to Stay with Your Pet*.

HOTELS

Hotels are the gold standard for lodging on the road. While they come in a wide range of categories, most hotels offer clean rooms with private baths and public areas that may include meeting rooms, bars, restaurants, gift shops, and exercise facilities. Large staffs are another hotel hallmark: doormen, valets, bellhops, a cleaning staff, room service, desk clerks, and concierges. In short, the advantages of a hotel are in the amenities and services it can provide. The staff can help you navigate an unfamiliar city. If you're wiped out from a long day's drive, you can treat yourself to a room-service dinner in bed. A hotel health club might offer massages to help work out the kinks that come from hours behind the steering wheel.

These services come at a price. Staying in high-caliber places can take a large bite out of your travel budget; a room in a top hotel can run several hundred dollars a night. Weigh the amenities offered against those you'd truly want or need. For instance, should you shell out $250 a night for a hotel with a famed late-night jazz lounge if you'll need to leave early the next day? Are you willing to haul your traveling gear along long corridors in order to have the views from a high-rise corner room? Should you splurge on an executive suite if you won't have much time for using its office and Internet facilities? You may decide to save the luxuries for a time when you'll have more leisure to enjoy them.

Suite Hotels

Many hotel chains now specialize in reasonably priced suites that consist of a living room and a bedroom. The privacy such a setup affords can be ideal for road trippers who need a bit of "alone time" after a long day in a car's close quarters. The separate bedroom can also allow the driver to catch up on sleep when others want to stay up to read or watch TV.

Resorts

Resort hotels are destinations unto themselves—and sometimes enough of an incentive to take a road trip in the first place. You might have access to a private beach, a spectacular golf course, or a full-service spa.

TO TIP OR NOT TO TIP?

Tipping is a major source of income for hotel employees. It's also a way for you to increase your chances of getting good service as a guest. Add a dollar or two to the following estimates for establishments that are in major cities or are especially high-end.

▶ **Bellhop:** Tip $1 or $2 per bag carried to and from your room.

▶ **Housecleaning:** Leave $1 to $2 each day. Leaving a daily tip ensures that the person who cleaned your room receives the gratuity. Otherwise, leave a total tip at the end of your stay, preferably in a marked envelope or with a note.

▶ **Room service:** Check to see if the gratuity is included in the bill. If not, 15%–20% of the total is appropriate. Even if the tip is included, it's a good idea to add a couple of dollars if you're satisfied with the service.

▶ **Concierge:** Securing dinner reservations or theater tickets merits $5 to $10 per service, and as much as $20 if the task was complicated or required at the last minute. Tip either at the time of service or at the end of your stay.

▶ **Doorman:** Holding the door is part of his job, but tip a buck or two for special attention, such as handling your luggage or hailing a cab.

▶ **Valet:** A dollar or two is appropriate each time a valet brings your car.

THE LITTLE EXTRAS

Hotels offer amenities that increase the cost of a room. Figure out which ones are important to you, and ask in advance if the hotel has them.

- ▶ **No-smoking rooms or floors**
- ▶ **Cable TV and/or pay-per-view movies**
- ▶ **Extra beds/cots/cribs**
- ▶ **Coffeemaker**
- ▶ **Refrigerator**
- ▶ **Minibar**
- ▶ **Room service**
- ▶ **Restaurant/bar on premises**
- ▶ **Wheelchair access**
- ▶ **Elevator**
- ▶ **Laundry service**
- ▶ **Baby-sitting**
- ▶ **Game room**
- ▶ **Exercise facilities**
- ▶ **Swimming pool**
- ▶ **Meeting rooms**
- ▶ **Business services**
- ▶ **In-room data port**
- ▶ **Valet parking**
- ▶ **Covered garage**

Maybe there's a casino on the ground floor, with all hotel guests receiving a set of chips to gamble away.

Although resorts can seem more expensive than ordinary hotels at first glance, their rates typically include more than just the room. The costs of meals, drinks, and activities might be bundled together. A stay at a spa resort, for instance, will likely include meals, use of the exercise facilities, and a choice of treatments. When you're calculating costs, remember that at many resorts, you won't need to spend additional money on dining, daytime activities, or evening entertainment.

What the Rating Systems Mean

Instead of using a single rating system that classifies lodgings throughout North America, travelers must rely on the judgments of several well-regarded organizations. Once you know what the ratings mean, you'll understand what to expect when the desk clerk tells you an inn earned four diamonds, or when a hotel's Web site touts its "SD" classification.

▶ AAA: The Automobile Association of America instituted its diamond ratings system in 1977, with establishments that meet the basic criteria of cleanliness and comfort earning one diamond and world-class properties earning five. A two-diamond hotel offers higher-quality furnishings than a one-diamond, while enhanced amenities and services earn a three-diamond rating.

▶ Mobil: The company rates lodgings on a scale from one to five stars, with one star denoting a clean, con-

Long hours in a car followed by nights in a strange bed can wreak havoc on your body. No matter what amenities your lodging has, you can make fitness a priority when you're on the road.

▶ **Hotel facilities:** Many larger hotels and better motel chains have swimming pools and exercise rooms on premises. Luxury resorts might even have golf courses, tennis courts, and hiking or walking trails in addition to pools and extensive fitness facilities. Moderate cardio workouts in particular can help refresh you for the day ahead.

▶ **Nearby exercise facilities:** If there aren't any exercise facilities in your hotel, ask at the front desk for directions to a nearby gym, pool, or a good, safe jogging route. If you belong to a gym at home, find out if they have reciprocal arrangements with other health club chains. Most gyms also offer day passes for visitors.

▶ **In-room exercise:** You can stay fit without any special facilities or equipment, without even leaving your hotel room. Push-ups, stretches, abdominal crunches, and wall squats can be done without any accoutrements. A briefcase or telephone book can serve as a small weight for arm or leg lifts. You can also bring travel dumbbells—these can be filled with water for a workout weight of a few pounds, then drained for packing.

venient establishment with limited services and five stars representing "consistently superlative service and expanded amenities." There are separate criteria for inns and hotels. A three-star hotel, for instance, has a minibar in each guest room, offers pay-per-view movies on television, and features valet parking. A three-star inn need not have valet parking but will have pay-per-view movies (or a VCR or DVD player) and a selection of beverages and snacks available, if not necessarily in a private minibar.

▶ Official Hotel Guide: This guide rates accommodations according to category—deluxe, first-class, and tourist—and quality. The ratings are frequently abbreviated as shown, with the appropriate code displayed on a hotel's brochures or Web site. Tourist class includes budget accommodations, first class covers basic full-service hotels, and deluxe comprises luxury properties. "Moderate" ratings indicate some less-than-satisfactory reviews, while "superior" indicates that the hotel surpassed the expectations within that category. The ratings are as follows: Superior Deluxe (SD), Deluxe (D), Moderate Deluxe (MD), Superior First Class (SF), First Class (F), Moderate First Class (MF), Superior Tourist (ST), Tourist (T), and Moderate Tourist (MT), plus Limited-Service First Class (LSF), which means the guest rooms are satisfactory but the public spaces are limited.

MOTELS

Motels are made for roadies on a budget. Most are conveniently located near major highways so you won't have to venture far off your route. They offer just what you require and not much more: a bed, a bath, and a place to park your car. And they cost far less than larger hotels.

A motel differs from a hotel in a few key respects. Motels, sometimes called motor lodges, generally offer free parking right outside your room, with rooms that have exterior access rather than interior hallways leading to a main lobby. Services are generally more limited than those in hotels, and dining may not be available.

When we go on a road trip, we always plan a special place to stay once we get there—someplace that feels comfortable and maybe a bit decadent, and someplace that has some flavor.

TRAVEL LOG But when we stop on the highway overnight on our way there, we're just looking for a place to sleep for a few hours, so we look for a motel that's part of a chain we've heard of. That way we figure we can at least trust that it'll be clean and in good condition.

—*Christina P., Aurora, Colorado*

Some motels do offer a few extras, such as cable TV or a pool. But they generally won't have amenities like health clubs or meeting rooms—and other than the daily cleaning staff, the front desk clerk will likely be the only staff you'll see.

Several motel chains stretch across the United States, with enough locations to ensure that you'll find one pretty much everywhere you go. The largest chains include Days Inn, Comfort Inn, EconoLodge, Motel 6, Super 8, and Travelodge. These large chains may lack local color but they're reliable and reserving rooms with them can be a cinch. Call a single toll-free reservations number, tell the operator where you're going and all the places you plan to stop along the drive, and you can book accommodations for your whole trip in one phone call.

GUEST HOUSES, INNS, AND B&BS

If character is paramount, the intimate accommodations of an inn, guest house, or bed-and-breakfast can enhance your trip. Although they exist in big cities, these privately owned lodgings are more frequently found in small towns, rural areas, or anywhere else people go to get away from it all.

All three types of lodgings offer similar amenities, though inns and guest houses sometimes have larger rooms and more upscale services, like aperitifs, afternoon tea, or limited business facilities. All feel homey for a good reason: The owners often live on premises, so the house really *is* a home. You should find a comfortable bedroom, but don't expect hotel amenities like in-room phones, TVs, or minibars. Some guest houses and B&Bs have rooms without private en-suite bathrooms; instead the bedrooms have shared bathrooms or private bathrooms down the hall. In those cases, you may want to bring a robe or other covering for the walk to the washroom.

People who treasure their privacy might be put off by the familiar interactions in these settings—communal meals, chatty hosts, and sometimes shared bathroom facilities. Yet it's not uncommon for guests to build friendly relationships with the people they meet during their stay. The hosts give you personal attention, and they can be a wonderful resource for local information.

At a B&B, the namesake meal might be a cold buffet with cereal, yogurt, fruit, bread, juice, and coffee. Or there might be more elaborate fare like scrambled eggs or pancakes. There won't be a menu of choices at most guest houses or B&Bs, but you won't leave hungry, and the cost of the meal is included in your room rate. Inns may have similar setups, or they may leave you to fend for yourself at breakfast. If so, your hosts can always recommend places to eat.

SHARED BATHROOMS As you would when visiting a friend's home, keep a few things in mind when using a B&B or guest house's shared bathroom. Don't leave your toiletries on the counter—keep them all in a toiletries kit you can take back and forth to your room. Leave the bathroom as neat as you found it, as a courtesy to your fellow guests; small accommodations can't have a maid clean the bathroom after every use. Budget extra time in the morning, in case you have to wait a few minutes for your turn in the shower—and when you're in the shower, be thoughtful of others and don't dawdle. If you're taking a hot shower, turn on the ventilation fan or open a window slightly so that the next person won't have to peer through the steam. And the cardinal rule: always knock before entering the bathroom and, once inside, lock the door.

BUDGET LODGINGS

Hostels are a popular option for young people traveling on a budget, who may place a higher value on meeting new people than on having privacy. Located in cities and near major tourist destinations, hostels usually provide dormitory-style accommodations that consist of a bunk bed in a room with several other guests of the same gender, and a bathroom down the hall. Blankets and pillows are provided, while other linens may be available for a small fee. Public areas generally include common kitchen, living room, and cafeteria space and may also include self-serve laundry facilities, a library, and an exercise area.

Tour and travel professionals often operate out of hostels, making excursions and day tours easy to arrange, and the fellow travelers you'll meet will be an invaluable source of information. Some hostels also offer private rooms and family accommodations.

If you plan on frequenting hostels during your trip, consider becoming a member of American Youth Hostels, which entitles you to receive discounts. But you can usually find a room if you're not a member, even if you're not a "youth" anymore.

You know the song, and the lyrics don't lie: It is fun to stay at the YMCA, for several reasons. They offer clean, comfortable rooms in major cities at a fraction of the price of an urban hotel. And YMCAs offer more than rooms; most have gyms, classes, and programs to enjoy during your stay. The accommodations are basic—typically a private bedroom with a shared bathroom down the hall. Think linoleum, not Persian rugs. But for value and location, the YMCA can't be beat.

TRAVEL LOG

People say you can't find anywhere cheap to stay in Manhattan, and they end up dropping 200 bucks a night to stay at second-rate hotels. Whenever I drive to New York, I stay at one of the YMCAs. They're right in the middle of the city, they've got gyms and pools, and they cost a quarter of most hotel rooms. With the money I save, I can take myself to a Broadway show and a nice dinner and still come out ahead.

–Lewis S., Washington, D.C.

Some Ys are open to men only, but others are open to women, and a few will accept families. Call ahead to make sure the YMCA you'd like to visit can accommodate you, and ask exactly what facilities that particular branch offers.

STAYING WITH FRIENDS OR FAMILY

There are some notable benefits to spending a night or two with friends or family. You'll save money, of course. But you'll also get more quality time with the people you love. You'll also have all the comforts of home—someone else's home, but a home nonetheless—so there's nothing to stop you if you want a drink of milk at 2 AM, need to borrow a clean T-shirt, or decide to skip the fancy restaurant in favor of a backyard barbecue.

There may be a downside to this rosy scenario, however. Sometimes, too much togetherness isn't a good thing. Do your former college roommate and his new wife really want you staying with them for a week, or are they just being polite? Is your sister's antiques-filled apartment a suitable place to bring your toddlers?

As a rule, you shouldn't stay more than three days in someone else's home. Always keep a backup option handy. That way, if things are not working out, you can tell your host, "We're going to move into a motel tomorrow, but we'd still like to spend our evenings with you if you're free."

Don't underestimate the personal strain involved in being a host. Try to keep your host's home looking as normal as possible and ask if there's anything house-related you should know. Every home has its particular quirks; for instance, you might need to use the shower a certain way or a door might have a tricky lock. It's better to ask than to learn the hard way or to inadvertently damage something. Keep your personal belongings in your bags, not strewn around the room. Make your bed in the morning, and clear your toiletries out of the bathroom unless it's a spare that's been designated especially for your use. Ask before you borrow anything. Also, don't expect your hosts to plan all of your activities and amusements for you. You may be on vacation but they likely won't be, and even when they're thrilled to see you, they'll need some time to themselves. Try to find out ahead of time what their schedules may be—which days are busiest, which evenings free—and take that into account when sketching out what you might like to do separately and together.

Bringing Your Own Supplies

A person's house is not a hotel. Ask in advance what you can bring. Your host might not have enough pillows, sheets, blankets, or towels for everyone in your party. Sleeping bags can be a lifesaver, especially for kids—they take up little room in your car and they're easy to roll up and put away. Adults might consider an inflatable mattress, which blows up in seconds and deflates easily to stow away. For between $40 and $100, these makeshift beds are more comfortable than cots, and they use standard-size sheets.

Thanking Your Host

Whether you're visiting Grandma or crashing on your best friend's sofa, you should offer thanks in a meaningful and sincere way. Bring a gift to your hosts, such as a lovely plant, a bottle of wine, or toys for their children. In addition, offer to treat them to dinner or spring for the tickets if you all go to an event together. A thank-you call or note is a must after you return home, and you can use this opportunity to send a gift if you didn't bring one during the visit.

SLEEP TIGHT

Finding the right place to spend the night on your road trip is as important as picking the right car and the right route. Choose wisely and you'll find places that suit both your budget and your lifestyle—and might even be as memorable as your days on the road.

ROAD RESOURCES

FODOR'S RESOURCES

Fodor's Gold Guides

Fodor's flagship series of guidebooks, covering destinations around the world. Each volume contains detailed information on hundreds of places to eat, sleep, and explore.

Fodor's Pocket Guides

Quick and easy guides to major cities.

Fodor's Road Guides USA

This series covers thousands of communities across the country, from big cities to small towns. Titles include *Great American Drives of the East, Great American Drives of the West*, and *Where to Stay with Your Pet*.

Fodor's Family Adventures

Profiles different types of soft adventures, discussing what each is like with kids of different ages, and recommends outfitters and trips. Each suggested trip comes with age-appropriateness rating.

Fodor's Healthy Escapes

Helps you choose among hundreds of spas and resorts across North America.

Fodor's How to Pack, Travel Fit & Healthy, Travel with Your Baby, Travel with Your Family, *and* How to Tip

Required reading for any traveler, these pocket-size books are packed with helpful information.

Fodors.com

This Web site is a great place to start planning your trip, with information on destinations, lodging, and restaurants. If you don't see what you are looking for, you can post questions in the Forum section and get a quick answer from the experts at Fodor's.

DESTINATIONS

Laboratory for Coastal Research
www.topbeaches.com

Site features listings and reviews of America's most pollution-free, beautiful beaches.

National Park Service
www.nps.gov
202/208–6843

Offers information kit on parks and monuments.

National Recreation Reservation Service
www.reserveusa.com
877/444–6777

Books services for everything from cabins to wilderness adventures.

National Scenic Byways
www.byways.org
800/4–BYWAYS

Free information, maps, and brochures available.

Recreational Opportunities on Federal Lands
www.recreation.gov

This information site is operated by a partnership among federal land-management bureaus. Select options on-line by choosing specific states, activities, and facilities.

TRANSPORTATION

Rental car agencies:

Advantage
www.arac.com
800/777–5500

Alamo
www.goalamo.com
800/327–9633

Avis
www.avis.com
800/331–1212

Budget
www.budget.com
800/527–0700

Dollar
www.dollar.com
800/800–4000

Enterprise
www.pickenterprise.com
800/325–8007

Hertz
www.hertz.com
800/654–3131

National
www.nationalcar.com
800/328–4567

Payless
www.paylesscarrental.com
800/237–2804

Rent-A-Wreck
www.rent-a-wreck.com
800/535–1391

Thrifty
www.thrifty.com
800/367–2277

Other vehicles:

Adventure Touring
www.adventuretouring.com
866/672–3572

Discount RV rental in the U.S. and Canada, plus motorcycle rental in the U.S.

Cruise America
www.cruiseamerica.com
800/327–7799

Nationwide RV rental organization also provides information on motorcycle rentals.

El Monte RV
www.elmonte.com
888/337–2214

Nationwide RV rental organization.

Go RVing Coalition
www.gorving.com
888/467–8464

Free information kit includes video with rental and travel tips, plus a list of RV dealers and campgrounds.

Harleys4rent.com
www.harleys4rent.com

Web site offers information on agencies that rent motorcycles—and not only Harley Davidsons, as the name might imply.

Moto-Directory.com
www.moto-directory.com

Provides links for various motorcycle-related topics, from competitions to women's issues.

Motorcycle Safety Foundation
www.msf-usa.org

Web site of this nonprofit organization covers information on training, safety, and more.

Recreation Vehicle Rental Association
www.rvra.org
800/366–0355

Directory of RV rental outlets covers more than 300 locations in the U.S. and Canada.

Ridetheworld.com
www.ridetheworld.com

On-line directory of motor-cycle rental outlets.

Roadside assistance:

American Automobile Association
www.aaa.com
212/757–2000

Members of the largest auto club in the U.S. receive 24-hour roadside assistance, travel-planning assistance, maps and directions, and a host of other services, plus discounts on accommodations and leisure activities.

Good Sam Club
www.goodsamclub.com
800/234–3450

Offers services for RVers, including roadside assistance, insurance, and travel information.

LUGGAGE

Eagle Creek Travel Gear
www.eaglecreek.com
760/471–7600

Manufactures sturdy gear like backpacks and duffels, with lifetime guarantees.

Eastern Mountain Sports
www.emsonline.com
888/463–6367

Outdoor gear retailer has on-line catalog and stores nationwide.

eBags
www.ebags.com
800/820–6126

Sells all types of luggage, including ergonomic designs.

Samsonite
www.samsonite.com
800/262–8282

Luggage manufacturer with product listing on request.

Sharper Image
www.sharperimage.com
800/344–5555

Sells innovative luggage and other travel gear.

Tumi
www.tumi.com
800/322–8864

Luggage manufacturer with nationwide stores and on-line catalog; its Tumi Tracer program adds identification tags to aid in recovering lost or stolen bags.

FOOD, FITNESS, AND OTHER ON-THE-ROAD INFO

Centers for Disease Control and Prevention
www.cdc.gov
General information:
800/311–3435

Travelers information:
800/394–8747

Fitscape
www.fitscape.com

Search on-line for health clubs convenient to anywhere you're headed.

Great Outdoor Recreation Page
www.gorp.com

Web site includes information to help you plan active vacations where you'll get plenty of exercise outside.

Radio-Locator
www.radio-locator.com

Search this site for info on radio station frequencies and formats all over the U.S. and Canada.

Roadfood by Jane and Michael Stern

This book's subtitle alone could make your mouth water; it promises to reveal the country's best ice cream, barbecue, diners, and more. The Sterns' other books, such as *Eat Your Way Across the U.S.A.,* also guide you to delicious local specialties. For their latest finds, look for their monthly column in *Gourmet* magazine.

Roadsideamerica.com
www.roadsideamerica.com

The authors of a pair of books on oddball tourist attractions across the U.S. have brought their finds to the Web. Search by state or topic for unusual points of interest, from wigwam motels to eclectic museums (Pez dispensers, lunch boxes).

The Tofu Tollbooth, 2nd edition by Elizabeth Zipern and Dar Williams
www.tofutollbooth.com

Folk singer Williams started this directory of eateries, grocery stores, and co-ops across the country that provide organic, vegetarian, and/or vegan food. A caveat: the book was last published in 1998, so call ahead to confirm an establishment is still open before going out of your way to find it.

U.S. Department of Agriculture
www.usda.gov

Check this site for information on foods that may not cross borders.

VegDining
www.vegdining.com

On-line guide to vegetarian restaurants everywhere.

TRAVEL WITH PETS

Dogfriendly.com
www.dogfriendly.com

On-line resource provides information about accommodations that accept dogs and how to travel with your pet to a wide range of destinations.

PetSmart
www.petsmart.com
888/839–9638

Nationwide retailer offers advice for traveling with your animal and sells any supplies you might need.

LODGING

Chain hotels and motels:

Best Western
www.bestwestern.com
800/528–1234

Clarion
www.clarioninn.com
800/252–7466

Comfort
www.comfortinn.com
800/228–5150

Courtyard by Marriott
www.courtyard.com
800/321–2211

Days Inn
www.daysinn.com
800/325–2525

Doubletree
www.doubletreehotels.com
800/222–8733

Drury Inns
www.druryinn.com
800/325–8300

EconoLodge
www.hotelchoice.com
800/555–2666

Embassy Suites
www.embassysuites.com
800/362–2779

Fairfield Inn by Marriott
www.fairfieldinn.com
800/228-2800

Fairmont Hotels
www.fairmont.com
800/527–4727

Four Seasons
www.fourseasons.com
800/332–3442

Friendship Inns
www.hotelchoice.com
800/453–4511

Hampton Inn
www.hampton-inn.com
800/426–7866

Hilton
www.hilton.com
800/445–8667

Holiday Inn
www.holiday-inn.com
800/465–4329

Howard Johnson
www.hojo.com
800/446–4656

Hyatt
www.hyatt.com
800/233–1234

Inns of America
www.innsofamerica.com
800/826–0778

Inter-Continental
www.interconti.com
800/327–0200

La Quinta
www.laquinta.com
800/531–5900

Loews
www.loewshotels.com
800/235–6397

Marriott
www.marriott.com
800/228–9290

Le Meridien
www.lemeridien.com
800/225–5843

Motel 6
www.motel6.com
800/466–8356

Omni
www.omnihotels.com
800/843–6664

Quality Inn
www.qualityinn.com
800/228–5151

Radisson
www.radisson.com
800/333–3333

Ramada
www.ramada.com
800/228–2828

Red Lion
www.redlion.com
800/547–8010

Red Roof Inn
www.redroof.com
800/843–7663

Renaissance
www.renaissancehotels.com
800/468–3571

**Residence Inn
by Marriott**
www.residenceinn.com
800/331–3131

Ritz-Carlton
www.ritzcarlton.com
800/241–3333

Sheraton
www.sheraton.com
800/325–3535

Signature Inns
www.signature-inns.com
800/822–5252

Sleep Inn
www.sleepinn.com
800/221–2222

Super 8
www.super8.com
800/848–8888

Travelodge
www.travelodge.com
800/255–3050

Westin Hotels & Resorts
www.westin.com
800/937–8461

**Wyndham Hotels
& Resorts**
www.wyndham.com
800/996–3426

Other accommodations:

Bedandbreakfast.com
www.bedandbreakfast.com

Web site allows you to search more than 27,000 B&Bs and inns around the world by location, amenities, or other criteria.

Best Holiday Trav-L-Park Association
www.best-holiday.com
800/323–8899

Campground chain.

Hostelling International–American Youth Hostels
www.hiayh.org
202/783–6161

Innplace.com
www.innplace.com

A directory of accommodations maintained by the Professional Association of Innkeepers International, a trade organization.

Kampgrounds of America
www.koa.com
800/588–2954

Campground chain.

Karen Brown's Guides
www.karenbrown.com

The on-line presence of longtime inns expert Karen Brown showcases the hand-selected inns in her books, which Fodor's publishes.

Leisure Systems, Inc./Yogi Bear's Jellystone Park Camp-Resorts
www.campjellystone.com
800/626–3720

Campground chain.

Spa Finder
www.spafinder.com
800/255–7727

World's largest spa travel company helps you search for spas and resorts and make reservations.

Spaquest
www.spa-quest.com
800/772–7837

Plan spa vacations and make reservations.

YMCA
www.ymca.net
212/308–2899

Web site has complete listing of all facilities offering residency and lists who is permitted to stay.

Rules of the Road

Alabama

License Requirements

To drive in Alabama you must be at least 16 years old and have a valid driver's license. Visitors who are at least 16 years old may drive with a valid license from their home state or country. Motorcycle operators must be licensed.

Right Turn on Red

Alabama allows right turns on red after making a full stop, unless otherwise posted.

Seat Belt and Helmet Laws

Alabama law requires all front-seat occupants to buckle up. In front and back seats, children under age six must occupy federally approved safety restraints. Four- and five-year-olds may use safety belts or the child safety seats required for younger children. Motorcyclists must wear helmets and shoes.

Speed Limits

Unless otherwise marked, Alabama's maximum speed limit is 70 mph on specified rural interstates, 65 mph on highways with four or more lanes, 55 mph on other highways, and 45 mph on county roads.

For More Information

Visit the Alabama Department of Transportation Web site at www.dot.state.al.us or call the Alabama State Troopers at 334/242–4400. Cellular phone users may call a nearby Alabama State Trooper by dialing *HP or *47.

Alaska

License Requirements

To drive in Alaska you must be at least 16 years old and have a valid driver's license. Visitors who are at least 16 years old may drive with a valid license from their home state or country. Motorcycle operators must be licensed.

Right Turn on Red

Alaska allows right turns on red after making a full stop, unless otherwise posted.

Seat Belt and Helmet Laws

In Alaska, all occupants of a vehicle must wear seat belts. Children under age four must occupy federally approved safety restraints. Helmets are mandatory for motorcyclists under age 19 and any motorcycle passengers.

Speed Limits

Unless otherwise marked, Alaska's maximum speed limits are 65 mph on specified highways and 55 mph on other roadways.

For More Information

Visit the Alaska Department of Motor Vehicles Web site at *www.state.ak.us/dmv* or call 907/269–5551.

Arizona

License Requirements

To drive in Arizona you must be at least 16 years old and have a valid driver's license from your home state or country.

Right Turn on Red

You may make a right turn on red after a full stop, unless there is a sign prohibiting it.

Seat Belt and Helmet Laws

If you are sitting in the front seat of any vehicle, the law requires you to wear your seat belt. Kids weighing between 4 and 40 pounds must be strapped into a federally approved safety seat. Anyone under the age of 18 is required to wear a helmet while riding on a motor-cycle.

Speed Limits

Speed limits in Arizona go as high as 75 mph but remain at 55 mph in heavily traveled areas. Be sure to check speed-limit signs carefully and often.

For More Information

Visit the Web site of the Arizona Department of Transportation's motor vehicles department at www.dot.state.az.us/MVD/mvd.htm, or call the Department of Public Safety at 602/223–2000.

Arkansas

License Requirements

Arkansas's graduated licensing system allows you to apply for a driver's license if you are 14 and can provide a birth certificate, proof of enrollment in school, and proof of grade point average of at least 2.0; a parent or legal guardian must accompany you to the testing site. When driving, an adult with a valid driver's license must be in the car with you. Valid out-of-state and foreign driver's licenses are good in Arkansas.

Right Turn on Red

A right turn on red at a traffic signal is permitted after you come to a full stop and yield to pedestrians and other traffic, unless a NO RIGHT TURN ON RED or similar sign is posted.

Seat Belt and Helmet Laws

State law requires all passengers to wear seat belts. All children under age five must wear safety restraints while the vehicle is in motion. Children under age four or weighing less than 40 pounds must be secured in an approved safety seat.

Speed Limits

Speed limits on major freeways range from 60 to 70 mph.

Other

Vehicle headlights must be turned on when windshield wipers are on.

For More Information

The Arkansas Department of Finance and Administration Web site, www.accessarkansas.org/dfa, includes replies for local driving FAQs. For information about road conditions, call the Arkansas Highway and Transportation Department at 501/569–2374.

California

License Requirements

You must be at least 16 years of age to get a driver's license in California. Persons with valid driver's licenses from other U.S. states and foreign countries are permitted to drive in the state.

Right Turn on Red

Unless otherwise posted, right turns on red are permitted after a full stop.

Seat Belt and Helmet Laws

All passengers are required to wear safety belts in the state of California. Children under four years of age or weighing less than 40 pounds must travel in an approved child safety seat. Motorcyclists must wear helmets.

Speed Limits

The maximum speed limit on California highways is 70 mph, unless otherwise posted.

For More Information

Check out the California Department of Motor Vehicles Web site, www.dmv.ca.gov, or call the California Highway Patrol at 916/657–7202.

Colorado

License Requirements

Drivers in Colorado must be at least 16 years old and have a valid driver's license; visitors at least 16 years old can drive with a valid license from their home state or country.

Right Turn on Red

A driver can legally turn right on a red light after coming to a full stop.

Seat Belt and Helmet Laws

State law requires automobile drivers and passengers in the front seat of the vehicle to use seat belts. Children under four years old and under 40 pounds, regardless of where in the vehicle they are riding, must use an approved safety seat.

Speed Limits

Individual speed limits are posted along all major thoroughfares and in all municipalities. The interstate system, except where posted for lower rates, maintains a 75-mph speed limit.

For More Information

The Colorado State Web site, www.colorado.gov, includes official driving regulations; you can also call the

Colorado State Patrol at 303/239–4500.

Connecticut

License Requirements

To drive in Connecticut you must be at least 16 years old and have a valid driver's license. Nonresidents age 16 and up can drive with a valid license from their home state. Residents of other countries may drive with a valid driver's license from their home countries if it is issued in English or if they have an international permit from their own country.

Right Turn on Red

You may make a right turn at a red light after coming to a full stop anywhere in the state unless a posted sign indicates otherwise.

Seat Belt and Helmet Laws

All drivers and front-seat passengers must wear seat belts. Children under the age of four must ride in a federally approved child-restraint system. Motorcyclists of any age must wear protective headgear.

Speed Limits

In 1998 Connecticut raised the speed limit from 55 mph to 65 mph on 334 mi of highway. Heavily traveled stretches of highway remain at 55 mph. Check posted speed limits carefully.

For More Information

Contact the State Department of Motor Vehicles at 800/842–8222 or on the Web at www.ct.gov/dmv.

Delaware

License Requirements

To drive in Delaware you must be at least age 16 and have a valid driver's license. Nonresidents age 16 and up can drive with a valid license from their home state or country.

Right Turn on Red

Drivers are permitted to make a right turn on red after coming to a full stop, unless otherwise posted.

Seat Belt and Helmet Laws

Seat belts are mandatory for all front-seat passengers in any vehicle. Children under 40 pounds or four years of age must travel in an approved safety seat. Motorcycle operators and passengers under 18 are required to wear helmets.

Speed Limits

Speed limits in Delaware are 55 mph on four-lane and major highways and 50 mph on two-lane roads. Speed limits may vary based on road conditions and/or specific areas, so always refer to posted signs.

For More Information

The state Web site, delaware.gov, includes links to the Office of Highway Safety and the Division of Motor Vehicles. You can also contact the Delaware State Police at 302/739–5931.

Florida

License Requirements

Drivers in Florida must be at least 16 years old and have a valid license. Licenses from other states or countries are acceptable.

Right Turn on Red

Unless posted otherwise, it is legal to take a right turn at a red light in clear traffic after a full stop.

Seat Belt and Helmet Laws

All automobile passengers must wear seat belts, and motorcycle riders must wear helmets.

Speed Limits

Speed limits are 55 mph on state highways, 30 mph within city limits and residential areas, and 55–70 mph on interstates and Florida's Turnpike, unless otherwise posted. Be alert for signs announcing exceptions.

For More Information

Call the Department of Highway Safety and Motor Vehicles at 850/922–9000 or check its Web site at www.hsmv.state.fl.us.

Georgia

License Requirements

To drive in Georgia, you must be at least 16 years old and have a valid driver's license. Licenses from other states or countries are acceptable.

Right Turn on Red

In Georgia, drivers can turn right on a red light after coming to a full stop, unless otherwise posted.

Seat Belt and Helmet Laws

A state law requires safety belts to be used by all persons riding in the front seat of a vehicle and all minors riding anywhere in the vehicle. Children ages three and four can use a regulation safety belt, but those age two and under must be restrained in an approved safety seat.

Speed Limits

Individual speed limits are posted in all municipalities. Most interstates maintain a 50-mph speed limit in metropolitan areas and a 70-mph limit in rural areas.

For More Information

Visit the Department of Motor Vehicle Safety Web site at www.dmvs.state.ga.us or call the Georgia Department of Transportation at 404/656–5267.

Hawai'i

License Requirements

To drive in Hawai'i, you must be at least 18 years old and have a valid driver's license. Licenses from other states or countries are acceptable.

Right Turn on Red

In Hawai'i, drivers can turn right on a red light after coming to a full stop, unless otherwise posted.

Seat Belt and Helmet Laws

State law requires safety belts to be used by all persons riding in the front seat of a vehicle and all minors riding anywhere in the vehicle. Children under four must be strapped into an approved safety seat. Motorcycle drivers or passengers under 18 must wear a helmet.

Speed Limits

Highway speed limits are usually 55 mph. Jaywalkers are common, so pay extra attention to pedestrians.

For More Information

Hawai'i does not have a statewide motor vehicles department, but you can visit the Web site of the state Department of Transportation at www.state.hi.us/dot or call the community relations office at 808/587–2160.

Idaho

License Requirements

To drive in Idaho you must be at least 16 years old and have a valid driver's license (15-year-olds may drive during daylight hours only). Visitors may drive with valid licenses from their home states or countries.

Right Turn on Red

Throughout the state, a right turn on red is permitted after a full stop, unless otherwise indicated by a sign.

Seat Belt and Helmet Laws

Drivers and front-seat passengers must wear seat belts. Children under the age of five must use a federally approved child safety seat. Only motorcyclists under the age of 18 are required to wear helmets.

Speed Limits

The speed limit on most interstate highways is 70 mph, except for portions of road that travel through urban or congested areas.

For More Information

Contact the Idaho Transportation Department Office of Public Affairs at 208/334–8005 or visit the state Division of Motor Vehicles Web site at www2.state.id.us/itd/dmv.

Illinois

License Requirements

Drivers must be at least 16 years old and have a valid driver's license from their home state or country.

Right Turn on Red

Right turn on red is permitted everywhere in the state except where posted.

Seat Belt and Helmet Laws

Seat belts must be worn by all drivers and front-seat passengers six years of age and over, even if the vehicle has air bags. Illinois does not have motorcycle-helmet laws, although riders are required to wear protective eyewear.

Speed Limits

The maximum speed limit in Illinois is 65 mph on rural interstate highways where posted. The maximum speed limit on most other highways is 55 mph.

For More Information

Contact the driver's services department at the office of the Illinois Secretary of State at 800/252–8980 or visit the Secretary of State's motorist services Web page at www.sos.state.il.us/publications/rr/rrtoc.html.

Indiana

License Requirements

Applicants for licenses in Indiana must be at least 18 years old; probationary licenses are available for people at least 16 years old. Visitors may drive with valid licenses from their home state or country.

Right Turn on Red

Throughout the state, a right turn on red is permitted after a full stop, unless otherwise indicated by a NO RIGHT TURN ON RED sign.

Seat Belt and Helmet Laws

Drivers and front-seat passengers must wear seat belts. Children under the age of five must use a federally approved child safety seat. Only motorcyclists under the age of 18 are required to wear helmets.

Speed Limits

The speed limit on most interstate highways is 65 mph, except for portions of road that travel through urban or congested areas. Watch for road signs, as the speed limit can change often and quickly.

For More Information

Contact the Indiana Bureau of Motor Vehicles at 317/233–6000 or on the Web at www.in.gov/bmv.

Iowa

License Requirements

To drive in Iowa, you must be at least 17 years old, although an instruction permit is possible at age 14 and an intermediate license may be granted at age 16. Nonresidents may drive with valid licenses from their home state or country.

Right Turn on Red

Right turns on red are allowed in Iowa after coming to a full and complete stop, unless otherwise posted.

Seat Belt and Helmet Laws

The driver and front-seat occupants must wear a seat belt. Children under the age of three are required to be in a safety seat. Children between the ages of three and six must either be in a safety seat or use a seat belt. Helmets are not required for motorcyclists.

Speed Limits

The speed limit on rural Iowa interstates is 65 mph. In urban areas and on secondary roads, the speed limit is 55 mph, unless otherwise posted. Drivers must reduce their speed when approaching a stationary, authorized vehicle with flashing lights, such as an emergency vehicle or a highway maintenance vehicle. Mopeds that operate over 25 mph are illegal in Iowa.

For More Information

Contact the Iowa Motor Vehicle Information Center 800/532–1121 or check the Web site at www.dot.state.ia.us/mvd.

Kansas

License Requirements

Residents of Kansas with a farm permit may drive as early as 14 years of age. However, other drivers must be at least 16 years old, have completed driver's training, and have a valid license from their state of residence.

Right Turn on Red

A right turn on red is allowed in Kansas after coming to a full and complete stop.

Seat Belt and Helmet Laws

All front-seat passengers, regardless of age, must wear a seat belt. All children under the age of four years must be in a safety seat. Motorcycle drivers or passengers are not required, but are encouraged, to wear a helmet.

Speed Limits

Speed limits on the open interstate or any separated multilane highway are 70 mph, on two-lane state high-

ways 65 mph, and on county roads 55 mph.

For More Information

Contact the Kansas Department of Transportation at 877/550–5368 or check out its Web site at www.ink.org/public/kdot.

Kentucky

License Requirements

A valid driver's license is required. Minimum age for drivers in Kentucky is 16. Visitors may drive with valid licenses from their home state or country.

Right Turn on Red

It's legal to turn right on red after a full stop throughout the state, unless otherwise posted.

Seat Belt and Helmet Laws

Seat belts are required by law, as are federally approved restraint seats for all kids under 40 inches tall. Helmets for motorcyclists are also required.

Speed Limits

On interstates and parkways, the speed limit is 65 mph. In metropolitan areas this decreases to 55 mph. If you are traveling on state roads, be aware that the limit through most towns is 35 mph.

For More Information

Check the Kentucky Transportation Cabinet Web site at www.kytc.state.ky.us or call 800/225–8747. For current road conditions on interstates, parkways, and other major routes, you can call 800/459–7623.

Louisiana

License Requirements

To drive in Louisiana, you must be at least 16 years old with a valid driver's license. Nonresidents may drive as long as they have a valid driver's license from their home state or country.

Right Turn on Red

Everywhere in the state you may make a right turn at a red light after a full stop, unless a posted sign prohibits it.

Seat Belt and Helmet Laws

All drivers and front-seat passengers must wear seat belts. Children under age 13 must wear a seat belt at all times, whether seated in front or back; children under age four must ride in a federally approved child safety seat. Motorcyclists may choose to ride without a helmet only if they are at least 21 years of age and carry a medical insurance policy with at least $10,000 in coverage. They are also required to keep their headlights and taillights on at all times.

Speed Limits

The maximum limits are 70 mph on interstate highways, 65 mph on controlled-access highways, 55 mph on state highways, and lower where posted.

For More Information

Visit the Louisiana Office of Motor Vehicles Web site at omv.dps.state.la.us or call the Louisiana State Police at 800/469–4828.

Maine

License Requirements

Anyone over the age of 16 with a valid driver's license, either resident or nonresident, may drive in Maine.

Right Turn on Red

Right turns on red are permitted throughout the state, unless otherwise posted.

Seat Belt and Helmet Laws

Seat belts are mandatory. While you cannot be stopped for not wearing one, you can be cited if stopped for another reason. Motorcycle helmets are required for drivers under 18 years of age and for those holding a license for under one year.

Speed Limits

The speed limit on I–95 (Maine Turnpike) is 65 mph, although it occasionally drops to 50 or 55 mph in more congested areas. Speed limits on U.S. 1 and state roads top out at 55 mph but can quickly change as you approach settled areas. The best bet is to keep alert. If not posted, the speed limit on back roads is 45 mph.

Other

A 1997 law requires motorists to have their headlights on any time their windshield wipers are in use or other weather conditions dictate. Headlights must also be on one half hour after sunrise and before sunset. Some Maine municipalities require cars to have snow tires in season. (All-season tires do not qualify.) Also, Maine has a tough drunk-driving policy.

For More Information

Contact the State Bureau of Highway Safety at 207/624–8756 or consult the Web site of the Bureau of Motor Vehicles at www.state.me.us/sos/bmv.

Maryland

License Requirements

To drive in Maryland you must be at least 16 years old and have a valid driver's license. Visitors may drive as long as they have valid licenses from their home state or country.

Right Turn on Red

Everywhere in Maryland you may make a right turn on red after a full stop, unless otherwise indicated.

Seat Belt and Helmet Laws

All drivers and front-seat passengers must wear seat belts. Children under four must ride in a federally approved child safety seat. All bicyclists and motorcyclists must wear helmets when riding on Maryland roads.

Speed Limits

In urban areas, particularly around Baltimore and heavily traveled I–95, the speed limit is 55 mph. On the interstates away from metropolitan areas, the speed limit is 60 or 65 mph.

For More Information

Maryland's state Web site, www.maryland.gov, and the State Highway Administration site, www.sha.state.md.us, have helpful driving information. You can also call the Department of Transportation at 888/713–1414.

Massachusetts

License Requirements

Drivers in Massachusetts must be at least 16 years old and must have a valid driver's license from their home state or country. Licensed Massachusetts drivers under age 18 cannot drive between midnight and 5 AM without a parent or guardian.

Right Turn on Red

Massachusetts allows right turns at red lights after coming to a complete stop and yielding to all pedestrians, unless otherwise posted. Note that most urban intersections, especially in Boston, are posted with NO RIGHT TURN ON RED signs, although not always conspicuously.

Seat Belt and Helmet Laws

Massachusetts law requires that everyone riding in a private passenger vehicle wear seat belts. State law also requires that motorcyclists and their passengers wear helmets.

Speed Limits

The maximum speed limit in Massachusetts, 65 mph, is only found along the interstates. On the more congested portions of the interstate system in and around Boston, the maximum is 50 to 55 mph. Numbered state highways have a maximum speed limit of 55 mph and are frequently posted much lower. Observe speed limits carefully, as speeding tickets are punitively expensive.

For More Information

Contact the Massachusetts Registry of Motor Vehicles at 617/351–4500 or visit its Web site, www.magnet.state.ma.us/rmv.

Michigan

License Requirements

Michigan's minimum driving age is 16 with a valid driver's license. Nonresidents age 16 and over may drive with a valid driver's license from their home state or country.

Right Turn on Red

Right turns on red are permitted throughout the state after a full stop, unless posted signs state otherwise.

Seat Belt and Helmet Laws

Seat belts are mandatory for all front-seat passengers and backseat passengers up to and including age 16. Children under four must be in an approved safety seat. Helmets are required for all motorcyclists.

Speed Limits

The speed limit on most Michigan roads and highways is 55 mph and 70 mph on freeways, unless otherwise posted. Watch signs carefully.

For More Information

Contact the state's Department of Transportation at 517/373–2090 or check the Michigan Web site, www.michigan.gov.

Minnesota

License Requirements

To drive in Minnesota, you must be at least 16 years old and have a valid driver's license. Visitors to the state may drive in Minnesota as long as they are at least 15 years old and have a valid license from their home state or country.

Right Turn on Red

Unless otherwise posted, you are permitted to make right turns on red after your vehicle has come to a complete stop.

Seat Belt and Helmet Laws

All drivers, front-seat passengers, and any other passengers ages 4 to 10 must wear seat belts. Children younger than four must ride in a federally approved safety seat. Motorcyclists must wear helmets.

Speed Limits

The speed limit on all interstate highways inside urban areas and on non-interstate freeways and expressways is 65 mph. The limit rises to 70 mph on interstates outside urban areas. In most other locations, the limit remains 55 mph.

For More Information

Contact the Minnesota Department of Public Safety at 651/282–6565 or check its Web site at www.dps.state.mn.us/dvs.

Mississippi

License Requirements

To drive in Mississippi, you must be at least 16 years old and have a valid driver's license. Visitors age 16 and up can drive with a valid license from their home state or country.

Right Turn on Red

Right turns are permissible on red unless otherwise posted.

Seat Belt and Helmet Laws

Seat belts are required for front-seat passengers and driver, and car seats are required for children under four. Motorcycle helmets are required.

Speed Limits

Unless otherwise posted, speed limits are 70 mph on interstate highways, 65 mph on non-limited access four-lane highways, 55 mph on other highways, and 50 mph on the Natchez Trace Parkway, where commercial trucking and hauling are prohibited. The Natchez Trace speed limit is particularly strictly enforced.

For More Information

Contact the Mississippi Department of Public Safety at 601/987–1212 or use its Web site, www.dps.state.ms.us.

Missouri

License Requirements

To drive in Missouri, you must be at least 16 years old and have a valid driver's license. Nonresidents age 16 and up can drive with a valid license from their home state or country.

Right Turn on Red

You may turn right on red anywhere in the state, *after* a full and complete stop, unless otherwise posted.

Seat Belt and Helmet Laws

Missouri requires all front-seat occupants in cars and persons under 18 years of age operating or riding in a truck to wear safety belts. Children ages 4 to 16 must be secured in a safety belt. All kids under age four must be in a child safety seat. Missouri requires all motorcycle riders to wear a helmet.

Speed Limits

The speed limit on most Missouri interstates is 70 mph, except where posted in and around large cities. The speed limit on state highways is 65 mph, except where posted. Be sure to check speed-limit signs carefully.

For More Information

Contact the State Department of Motor Vehicles 573/526–3669 or go to the Web site, www.dor.state.mo.us/mvdl.

Montana

License Requirements

Montana recognizes valid driver's licenses from other states and countries. The minimum driving age is 15 with driver training or 16 without.

Right Turn on Red

Right turns on red are allowed, unless otherwise posted.

Seat Belt and Helmet Laws

The driver and all passengers in motor vehicles on Montana roadways must wear seat belts. Law-enforcement officers will not pull you over if you're not wearing a seat belt, but they will ticket you if you commit other infractions while unbelted. Children two and younger must be in a federally approved child restraint device. Children ages two to

four who weigh no more than 40 pounds must also be secured in a child restraint device. All motorcycle riders under 18 years of age must wear a helmet in Montana.

Speed Limits

The maximum speed on the state's interstate highways is 75 mph; non-interstate roadway limits are 70 mph daytime and 65 mph at night. Trucks over 1-ton capacity have interstate speed limits of 65 mph and non-interstate limits of 60 mph daytime and 55 mph at night.

For More Information

Contact the Montana Highway Patrol at 406/444–3780 or on-line at www.doj.state.mt.us/mhp.

Nebraska

License Requirements

General driver's licenses are available at age 16, though some special permits for resident youth are allowed. Visitors age 16 and up can drive with a valid license from their home state or country.

Right Turn on Red

Unless otherwise posted, right turns on red are permitted after a full stop. Left turns on red are allowed where such a turn would not cross an oncoming traffic lane.

Seat Belt and Helmet Laws

Seat belts are required of the driver and all front-seat passengers. Children under age five or weighing less than 40 pounds must be secured in a car seat that meets federal guidelines. All motorcycle operators and passengers must wear approved motorcycle helmets.

Speed Limits

Limits on interstates are 75 mph except in metropolitan areas around Lincoln and Omaha. State highways speed limits are generally 60 mph; some stretches are 55 mph. County road limits are generally 55 mph, 50 mph on unpaved county roads.

For More Information

Contact the Nebraska State Patrol at 402/471–4545, the Emergency Highway Help Line at 800/525–5555, or the Department of Motor Vehicles at 402/471–2281. Nebraska's state Web site, www.nol.org , links to helpful information on safety, road conditions, and the like.

Nevada

License Requirements

To drive in Nevada you must be at least 16 and have a valid driver's license from your home state or country.

Right Turn on Red

Right turns on red are permitted everywhere.

Seat Belt and Helmet Laws

All drivers and front-seat passengers must wear seat belts. Children under 10 must wear a seat belt at all times; children under 4 must ride in child seats. Motorcyclists and passengers are required to wear helmets at all times.

Speed Limits

Some places on I–80 and I–15 you can drive 75 mph. Other places, and on the U.S. highways, the speed limit is 70 mph. It's a quick 65 mph on the interstates in the heart of Las Vegas and Reno.

For More Information

Contact the Nevada Department of Motor Vehicles at 702/486–4368 or on-line at www.dmvnv.com.

New Hampshire

License Requirements

To drive in New Hampshire you must be at least 16 years old and have a valid driver's license from your home state or country.

Right Turn on Red

Everywhere in the state, you can make a right turn at a red light *after* a complete stop unless the intersection is posted to the contrary.

Seat Belt and Helmet Laws

Children under 12 must wear seat belts or approved restraints. Motorcycle helmets are required for riders under 18.

Speed Limits

Most interstates have speed limits of 65 mph, except in congested areas where the limit is 55 mph. Secondary roads rarely have speed limits over 50 mph.

For More Information

Contact the New Hampshire Department of Safety at 603/271–2333 or on-line at www.state.nh.us/safety.

New Jersey

License Requirements

To drive in New Jersey you must be at least 17 years old and have a valid driver's license. Visitors may drive as long as they have a valid license from their home state or country.

Right Turn on Red

Everywhere in the state you may make a right turn at a red light after a full stop unless otherwise posted.

Seat Belt and Helmet Laws

All drivers and front-seat passengers must wear seat belts. Children under age 10 must wear a seat belt at all times, whether they are in the back or the front. Children under age four must be in a federally approved child safety seat. Motorcyclists must wear helmets and are required to keep their headlights and taillights on at all times.

Speed Limits

New Jersey is testing a 65-mph speed limit on some major highways. In areas of heavier traffic, though, 55 mph is still the speed limit. Speed limits often change from town to town, so be sure to check the speed-limit signs carefully.

Other

Headlights must be on whenever windshield wipers are on.

For More Information

Contact the State Department of Transportation at 609/292–6500 or on-line at www.state.nj.us/transportation.

New Mexico

License Requirements

Provisional licenses can be granted to people at least 16 years old. Visitors must have a valid driver's license from their home state or country.

Right Turn on Red

A driver can turn right on a red light after coming to a full stop.

Seat Belt and Helmet Laws

A state law requires automobile drivers and passengers to use seat belts. Although bikers are not required by law to wear helmets, they are strongly urged to do so. Children riding in automobiles must be restrained in the backseat, and if they are age four or under, they must be restrained in a children's car seat secured in the backseat.

Speed Limits

Individual speed limits are posted in all municipalities. Most interstates maintain a 75-mph speed limit, depending on location.

For More Information

Contact the New Mexico Highway Hotline at 800/432–4269. The state Web site, www.state.nm.us, can link you to the Motor Vehicle Division and the Highway and Transportation Department.

New York

License Requirements

Licensed 16-year-olds may drive, with restrictions. Those 18 and older have no restrictions. In New York City, you must be 18 or older to drive, even with a valid out-of-state license.

Right Turn on Red

Right turns on red are permitted in most areas, unless otherwise posted; they are not allowed in New York City.

Seat Belt and Helmet Laws

Seat belts are required for driver, front-seat passengers, and backseat passengers between the ages of 4 and 10. Children younger than four must be in child restraints. Motorcyclists are required to wear helmets.

Speed Limits

Maximum limits are 65 mph on rural interstates, 55 mph on nonrural interstates. Watch signs on all roads.

For More Information

Contact the State Police Headquarters at 518/457–6811 or 800/842–2233 or visit the state Department of Motor Vehicles on-line at www.nydmv.state.ny.us.

North Carolina

License Requirements

To drive without restrictions in North Carolina you must be at least 18 years old and have a valid driver's license. Provisional licenses are granted for drivers at least 16 years old. Visitors who are at least 16 can drive with a valid license from their home state or country.

Right Turn on Red

Everywhere in the state you can make a right turn at a red light after a full stop.

Seat Belt and Helmet Laws

All drivers and front-seat passengers must wear a lap safety belt or lap and shoulder belt, whichever the seat-ing position provides. All children between the ages of 5 and 12 must wear a belt. Children age five and under and less than 40 pounds must be properly secured in a weight-appropriate child restraint system. Motorcyclists are required to wear helmets and to keep their headlights and taillights on at all times.

Speed Limits

On main roads outside urban areas, the maximum speed is 55 mph, and on interstates it's 70 mph. Speed-limit signs change rather abruptly, though, so stay alert.

For More Information

Contact the state's Division of Motor Vehicles at 919/715–7000 or on-line at www.dmv.dot.state.nc.us.

North Dakota

License Requirements

The minimum driving age in North Dakota is 16. You may not drive in North Dakota if you are under 16, even if you are licensed in another state.

Right Turn on Red

You may turn right on a red light after stopping when the intersection is clear of both pedestrians and vehicles, unless otherwise posted.

Seat Belt and Helmet Laws

North Dakota law requires all front-seat occupants to wear safety belts. Children under age three& must be properly secured in an approved child restraint seat, and children ages 3 to 10 must be properly secured in either an approved child restraint seat or a safety belt. North Dakota does not have a motorcycle helmet law.

Speed Limits

The speed limit is 70 mph on interstate highways, except when otherwise posted around major cities. On all other primary and secondary highways, the speed limit is 65 mph unless otherwise posted. Many roads require a slightly lower speed at night.

For More Information

Contact the North Dakota Department of Transportation at 701/328–2500 for general information or 701/328–7623 for road reports; the Web site is www.state.nd.us/dot.

Ohio

License Requirements

Sixteen- and 17-year-olds who have completed drivers' education classes can obtain probationary licenses; otherwise, drivers must be 18. Visitors age 16 and up can drive with a valid license from their home state or country.

Right Turn on Red

Unless posted otherwise, it is legal to make a right turn at a red light after a full stop.

Seat Belt and Helmet Laws

Drivers and front-seat passengers must wear seat belts. Kids under age four or less than 40 pounds must use a child-safety restraint. Motorcyclists under age 18 or with less than one year's driving experience must wear helmets.

Speed Limits

Speed limits are 55 mph on township, county, and state roads and 55 to 65 mph on expressways and the Ohio Turnpike.

For More Information

Call the Ohio Bureau of Motor Vehicles at 800/589–8247 or check on-line at www.state.oh.us/odps/division/bmv.

Oklahoma

License Requirements

Graduated driver's licenses are available for applicants who are at least 16 years old. Nonresident licenses are honored for drivers at least 16 years old.

Right Turn on Red

Right turns on red are permitted throughout the state after a complete stop, unless otherwise posted.

Seat Belt and Helmet Laws

Seat belts are mandatory for drivers and front-seat passengers; child restraints are mandatory for children under four years of age. Children four and five years old must use child restraints or seat belts at all times. Safety helmets are required for motorcyclists under age 18; face shields, goggles, or windscreens are mandatory. Motorcyclists are required to use their headlights at all times, even during daylight hours.

Speed Limits

Speed limits are 70 mph on four-lane or divided highways, 75 mph on turnpikes, and 55 mph on county roads. Residential and business-district limits are set by local ordinance; watch for posted signs.

For More Information

Contact the Oklahoma Department of Public Safety at 405/425–2424 or on-line at www.dps.state.ok.us.

Oregon

License Requirements

To drive in Oregon, you must be at least 16 years old and hold a valid driver's license. Visitors may drive as long as they hold a valid license from their home state or country.

Right Turn on Red

A right turn may be made onto a two-way street after stopping at a red light and yielding as necessary, unless otherwise prohibited by a sign. When entering a one-way street, you may turn right or left with the movement of the traffic after stopping for the red light and yielding as necessary.

Seat Belt and Helmet Laws

Safety-belt use is mandatory for all drivers and passengers. Children under four who weigh 40 pounds or less are required to be in an approved child safety seat. All motorcycle operators and passengers are required to wear helmets.

Speed Limits

The maximum speed limit in any city and on urban interstates and highways is 55 mph, while on rural interstate highways it is 65 mph.

For More Information

Contact Oregon Driver and Motor Vehicles Services at 503/945–5000 or visit its Web site at www.oregondmv.com. The Oregon Department of Transportation Web site, www.odot.state.or.us, includes road reports.

Pennsylvania
License Requirements

To drive in Pennsylvania, you must be at least 16 years old and have a valid driver's license. Visitors at least 16 years old can drive as long as they have a valid driver's license issued in their home state or country.

Right Turn on Red

Everywhere in Pennsylvania, you can make a right turn on red after coming to a complete stop, unless a sign is posted prohibiting it.

Seat Belt and Helmet Laws

Seat belts are required for all passengers in the front seat. Children age four and older can use a regulation seat belt. Children under four years old must be in an approved passenger restraint everywhere in the vehicle and must use an approved safety seat in the front seat. Children ages one to three can use a regulation seat belt in the backseat only; under age one, an approved safety seat must be used everywhere in the vehicle.

Speed Limits

The speed limit is 65 mph on rural interstate highways and 55 mph on heavily congested highways in and around urban areas.

For More Information

Contact Pennsylvania's Driver and Vehicle Services at 717/391–6190 or on-line at www.dmv.state.pa.us.

Rhode Island
License Requirements

To drive in Rhode Island you must be at least 16 years old and have a valid driver's license. Visitors may drive as long as they have a valid license from their home state or country.

Right Turn on Red

Right turns on red are permitted after a complete stop, unless prohibited by sign.

Seat Belt and Helmet Laws

Seat belts are required for all operators and passengers. All children under age five must ride in the backseat. Helmets are not required for operators of motorcycles but are required for passengers. Protective goggles, glasses, or windscreen are required of operators and passengers.

Speed Limits

The maximum legal speed in Rhode Island is 65 mph on major roads, or as posted.

For More Information

Contact the Division of Motor Vehicles at 401/588–3020 or on-line at www.dmv.state.ri.us.

South Carolina

License Requirements

South Carolina's minimum driving age is 16 with a valid driver's license. Licenses for those under age 17, however, include some restrictions. Visitors may drive with a valid license from their home state or country.

Right Turn on Red

Everywhere in the state, you can make a right turn at a red light after a full stop, unless a posted sign forbids it.

Seat Belt and Helmet Laws

All persons in the front seat of a moving vehicle must wear safety belts. Children six years of age and younger must be secured in a federally approved child safety seat. All persons under age 21 must wear a helmet while riding a motorcycle in South Carolina.

Speed Limits

The maximum speed allowed on South Carolina highways is 55 mph unless otherwise noted.

Other

South Carolina has a headlight law: If windshield wipers are on because of weather conditions, headlights must also be on.

For More Information

Contact the State Department of Motor Vehicles at 803/737–4000 or on-line at www.scdps.org/dmv.

South Dakota

License Requirements

To drive in South Dakota, you must be at least 14 years old and have a valid driver's license. Visitors at least 16 years old may drive as long as they possess a valid license from their home state or country.

Right Turn on Red

Unless otherwise posted, you may make a right turn on red after a full stop everywhere in the state. Exceptions include one-way streets in downtown Rapid City, which are posted.

Seat Belt and Helmet Laws

All drivers and front-seat passengers under 17 years of age must wear a seat belt. Children under age five may only ride in a federally approved child safety seat, or if they exceed 40 pounds, the child may be secured with a seat belt. Motorcyclists 18 and older are not required to wear a helmet in South Dakota. Minors riding or driving a motorcycle must wear a helmet. Eye protection is required for all motorcyclists. It is recommended that all motorcyclists have headlights and taillights on at all times.

Speed Limits

In 1995, South Dakota raised its speed limit to 75 mph on its two interstates, except as noted near Rapid City and Sioux Falls. Posted limits on state and secondary highways are usually 65 mph, although most Black Hills scenic roadways are set at 55 mph.

For More Information

Contact the South Dakota Office of Driver Licensing at 605/773–6883 or its Web site at www.state.sd.us/dcr for information on licenses and highway safety; check the Highway Patrol site, hp.state.sd.us, for road reports.

Tennessee

License Requirements

You must be 16 years of age to get a driver's license in Tennessee. Persons with a valid driver's license issued in another U.S. state or a foreign country are permitted to drive in Tennessee.

Right Turn on Red

Unless otherwise posted, you are permitted to make right turns on red in the state of Tennessee.

Seat Belt and Helmet Laws

All front-seat passengers are required to wear safety belts. Children under four must travel in a child restraint device that meets Federal Motor Vehicle Safety Standards. Motorcyclists must wear helmets.

Speed Limits

The speed limit on rural Tennessee interstates is 70 mph; speed limits on metro-area interstates are regulated by the specific metro area—watch for signs. The speed limit on major highways is 55 mph, unless otherwise indicated on highway signs.

Other

Headlights must be used during foggy or otherwise inclement weather.

For More Information

For information on road conditions, call 800/342–3258. For license and regulations information, visit the Web site www.state.tn.us/drive.html.

Texas

License Requirements

To drive in Texas you must be at least 16 years old and have a valid driver's license. Visitors may drive as long as they have a valid license from their home state or country.

Right Turn on Red

You may make a right turn on red after a full stop anywhere in the state, unless otherwise posted.

Seat Belt and Helmet Laws

All drivers and front-seat passengers must wear seat belts. Children under age four must wear a seat belt, whether seated in the front or back. Children under age two must only ride in a federally approved child safety seat. Motorcyclists under age 21 must wear a helmet; motorcyclists age 21 and over are not required to wear a helmet if they have proof of insurance valued over $10,000 or have proof of completion of a motorcycle operations course.

Speed Limits

The speed limit in Texas is 70 mph. In heavily traveled corridors, though, the limit is 55. Be sure to check speed-limit signs carefully.

For More Information

Contact the Texas Department of Public Safety at 512/424–2000 or on-line at www.txdps.state.tx.us.

Utah

License Requirements

The minimum driving age in Utah is 16. All drivers must have a valid driver's license. Visitors may drive in Utah as long as they have a valid driver's license and are at least 16 years old.

Right Turn on Red

Right turns are allowed on a red light after the vehicle has come to a complete stop, unless otherwise posted.

Seat Belt and Helmet Laws

Utah law requires seat-belt use for drivers, front-seat passengers, and all children under 10. Children under the age of two are required to be in federally approved safety seats. Helmet use is mandatory for motorcyclists and passengers under the age of 18.

Speed Limits

On major highways the speed limit is 55 mph, particularly in urban areas. Speed limits increase to 65 or 75 mph on interstate highways in rural areas, but watch out: "rural areas" are determined by census boundaries, so their delineation may seem arbitrary to the casual driver. Transition zones from one speed limit to another are indicated with pavement markings and additional signs.

For More Information

Contact the Utah Department of Transportation at 801/965–4518 or on-line at www.sr.ex.state.ut.us.

Vermont

License Requirements

Valid licenses issued by other state and national jurisdictions are recognized in Vermont. The legal driving age is 16.

Right Turn on Red

Right turns on red are permitted throughout the state unless posted signs indicate otherwise.

Seat Belt and Helmet Laws

Vermont law requires all vehicle occupants to be secured with seat belts; children under the age of five must be secured in a federally approved child safety seat. Motorcycle operators and passengers are required to wear helmets.

Speed Limits

The limit on Vermont highways is 50 mph, except as posted otherwise in settled areas; on interstate highways, a 65-mph speed limit is observed unless posted otherwise.

For More Information

Contact the Vermont Department of Motor Vehicles at 802/863–7292 or on-line at www.aot.state.vt.us/dmv.

Virginia

License Requirements

To drive in Virginia you must be at least 16 years old and have a valid driver's license from your home state. Residents of Canada and most other countries may drive here as long as they have a valid license from their home country.

Right Turn on Red

In most places, drivers may make a right turn on a red light after coming to a full stop. The practice is prohibited in some metropolitan areas, however; watch for signs at intersections with traffic lights.

Seat Belt and Helmet Laws

Seat belts are required for drivers and front-seat passengers; restraints are required for children under the age of four. Helmets are required for motorcyclists,

as are a face shield or safety goggles or an approved windshield.

Speed Limits

The maximum speed limit on most of Virginia's interstates is 65 mph. In heavily traveled corridors, however, the speed limit is 55 mph. Check speed-limit signs carefully.

For More Information

Call the State Department of Motor Vehicles headquarters in Richmond at 866/368–5463 or visit the Web site at www.dmv.state.va.us.

Washington

License Requirements

In Washington, drivers must be at least 16 years old, possess a valid driver's license, and carry proof of insurance. (Uninsured cars may be impounded.) Visitors age 16 and up may drive with a valid driver's license from their home state or country.

Right Turn on Red

Right turns on red are permitted throughout the state unless posted signs state otherwise.

Seat Belt and Helmet Laws

Seat belts are mandatory for the driver and for all passengers. Children under 40 pounds must be strapped into approved safety seats. Motorcyclists must wear helmets.

Speed Limits

Speed limits on highways and interstates vary from 60 to 70 mph. Check posted signs for pertinent limits.

For More Information

Call the Department of Transportation at 360/705–7000 or check the Web sites of the Department of Licensing at www.dol.wa.gov and the Department of Transportation at www.wsdot.wa.gov.

West Virginia

License Requirements

You must be at least 16 years old and have a valid license to drive in West Virginia. Nonresidents at least 16 years old can drive here with a valid license from their home state or country.

Right Turn on Red

Right turns on red lights are allowed throughout the state, unless otherwise posted.

Seat Belt and Helmet Laws

Seat belts are required for all front-seat occupants and backseat passengers under 18; child restraints are required for kids under two years old. Helmets are mandatory for both motorcycle drivers and passengers.

Speed Limits

The speed limit on interstate highways is 70 mph and 55 mph on most major state routes. Be sure to check locally posted signs.

For More Information

Contact the West Virginia Department of Transportation at 800/642–9066 or online at www.wvdot.com.

Wisconsin

License Requirements

To drive in Wisconsin, you must be at least 16 years old and have a valid driver's license. Nonresidents may drive as long as they have a valid license from their home state or country.

Right Turn on Red

In most of Wisconsin you can make a right turn at a red light after coming to a full stop, unless posted signs state otherwise.

Seat Belt and Helmet Laws

Drivers and passengers must wear seat belts at all times. Children under age four must use a federally approved child safety seat. Motorcyclists under 18 are required to wear helmets and eye protection; adults are not required to do so.

Speed Limits

Speed limits in Wisconsin vary widely. On expressways they can range from 50 to 65 mph, and on highways from 40 to 55 mph. Be sure to check signs carefully.

For More Information

Contact the Department of Transportation, Division of Motor Vehicles at 414/266–1000 or on-line at www.dot.state.wi.us/dmv.

Wyoming

License Requirements

To drive in Wyoming you must be at least age 16 and have a valid driver's license. Nonresidents age 16 and up can drive in Wyoming with a valid license from their home state or country.

Right Turn on Red

Right turns on red are allowed throughout the state unless posted otherwise.

Seat Belt and Helmet Laws

Drivers and front-seat passengers must wear seat belts; children under four years old and/or under 40 pounds must be seated in a federally approved safety seat. Motorcyclists are not required by law to wear helmets, but minors must wear a helmet when on a motorcycle. Also, motorcyclists must have their headlights on at all times.

Speed Limits

Wyoming was one of the first states to adopt higher speed limits when federal authorities allowed it in 1995. Limits are 65 mph on state highways and 75 mph on interstate highways for all vehicles.

For More Information

Contact the Wyoming Department of Transportation at 307/777–4800; the department also maintains a driver services Web site at dot.state.wy.us/web/driver_services.

Index

P

R

Fodor's
Key to the Guides

America's guidebook leader publishes guides for every kind of traveler. Check out our many series and find your perfect match.

Fodor's Gold Guides
America's favorite travel-guide series offers the most detailed insider reviews of hotels, restaurants, and attractions in all price ranges, plus great background information, smart tips, and useful maps.

Fodor's Road Guide USA
Big guides for a big country—the most comprehensive guides to America's roads, packed with places to stay, eat, and play across the U.S.A. Just right for road warriors, family vacationers, and cross-country trekkers.

COMPASS AMERICAN GUIDES
Stunning guides from top local writers and photographers, with gorgeous photos, literary excerpts, and colorful anecdotes. A must-have for culture mavens, history buffs, and new residents.

Fodor's CITYPACKS
Concise city coverage with a foldout map. The right choice for urban travelers who want everything under one cover.

Fodor's EXPLORING GUIDES
Hundreds of color photos bring your destination to life. Lively stories lend insight into the culture, history, and people.

Fodor's POCKET GUIDES
For travelers who need only the essentials. The best of Fodor's in pocket-size packages for just $9.95.

Fodor's To Go
Credit-card–size, magnetized color microguides that fit in the palm of your hand—perfect for "stealth" travelers or as gifts.

Fodor's FLASHMAPS
Every resident's map guide. 60 easy-to-follow maps of public transit, parks, museums, zip codes, and more.

Fodor's CITYGUIDES
Sourcebooks for living in the city: Thousands of in-the-know listings for restaurants, shops, sports, nightlife, and other city resources.

Fodor's AROUND THE CITY WITH KIDS
68 great ideas for family days, recommended by resident parents. Perfect for exploring in your own backyard or on the road.

Fodor's ESCAPES
Fill your trip with once-in-a-lifetime experiences, from ballooning in Chianti to overnighting in the Moroccan desert. These full-color dream books point the way.

Fodor's FYI
Get tips from the pros on planning the perfect trip. Learn how to pack, fly hassle-free, plan a honeymoon or cruise, stay healthy on the road, and travel with your baby.

Fodor's Languages for Travelers
Practice the local language before hitting the road. Available in phrase books, cassette sets, and CD sets.

Karen Brown's Guides
Engaging guides to the most charming inns and B&Bs in the U.S.A. and Europe, with easy-to-follow inn-to-inn itineraries.

Baedeker's Guides
Comprehensive guides, trusted since 1829, packed with A–Z reviews and star ratings.

At bookstores everywhere.   www.fodors.com/books

Notes

Notes

_____

_____

_____

_____

_____

_____

_____

_____

_____

_____

_____

_____

Notes

_____

_____

_____

_____

_____

_____

_____

_____

_____

_____

_____

_____